A NORTON MUSIC ANTHOLOGY

*The Solo Song*

1580-1730

# The Solo Song

## 1580-1730

A NORTON MUSIC ANTHOLOGY

Edited by Carol MacClintock

UNIVERSITY OF CINCINNATI

W · W · NORTON & COMPANY · INC · NEW YORK

M
1619
. M 17
. S 6

Copyright © 1973 by W. W. Norton & Company, Inc.

FIRST EDITION
Library of Congress Cataloging in Publication Data

MacClintock, Carol Cook, 1910–     comp.
    The solo song, 1580–1730.

    (A Norton music anthology)
    Words in Italian, French, German, and/or English;
    figured bass realized for keyboard instrument.
    Bibliography: p.
    1. Songs.  2.  Songs—History and criticism.
I.   Title.
M1619.M17S6        784'.3        70–146039
ISBN 0–393–09982–2

PRINTED IN THE UNITED STATES OF AMERICA

1 2 3 4 5 6 7 8 9 0

# Contents

## Part I: Songs by Italian Composers

## Part II: Songs by English Composers

## Part III: Songs by French Composers

## Part IV: Songs by German Composers

# Foreword

The present volume is the outgrowth of my experience in conducting a graduate class in the music of the late Renaissance and Baroque eras. Examples of instrumental music and opera were fairly easily accessible in published form, but the solo song, an almost completely neglected area, could be found almost exclusively in early prints, in manuscript, or in unrealized form in some of the learned publications. I nearly always had to make my own transcriptions and realizations of the pieces I wanted to use. In the course of time I came to the conclusion that there was a wealth of fine music almost inaccessible to the singer and the scholar. Other scholars with whom I discussed the problem or who learned of my activities had had the same difficulties and gave me every encouragement to bring out an anthology which would fill a serious lacuna and make available some of this literature in usable form.

I wish to acknowledge the interest and helpfulness of David Burrows, who provided several Cesti cantatas, of Owen Jander, who gave me access to his Stradella manuscripts, of Sven Hansell, who sent the Hasse cantata, and of Erich Schwandt, who made many excellent suggestions, sent numerous pieces for my consideration, and provided the realization of the Moreau *cantique*. I should mention also that my husband, Professor Lander MacClintock, was a great help in providing translations of the texts. Last but not least, I wish to thank the members of my classes and Collegium Musicum who gave many of these compositions a trial run.

*Carol MacClintock*

# Introduction

It is abundantly obvious that the historian of music cannot stick a pin in a calendar or an atlas and say "at this time and in this place solo song in West Europe came into being." Almost as difficult would it be to attempt an explanation of the extraordinary flowering of the art song for single voice that took place in Western Europe between approximately 1575 and 1700, yet any work of art is at the same time both the culmination of a development and the beginning of another, not an isolated or inexplicable phenomenon. The song for solo voice has always existed; the accompanied song for solo voice has flourished since the days of the troubadours and there have been brilliant vocal moments in the course of history—the exquisite, sophisticated ballades and virelais of Machaut, the delicate quattrocento madrigals and ballate, the courtly chansons of Dufay and Binchois are but a few of the masterpieces of vocal art. However, in 16th-century Italy the concern of composers for expressiveness, for dramatic declamation, brought about an epoch-making change in the style and art of singing. Evidence of this change is to be observed first in the Italian polyphonic *frottole* of the first quarter of the century which could be sung either as part-songs or as accompanied vocal solos. Airs for solo voice and lute also became fashionable at about the same time, as we learn from poems, essays, and accounts such as those in Castiglione's *The Courtier,* and there is clear evidence that a specific literature for solo voice was coming into being. Unfortunately, few examples of songs written before 1550 exist and these are found chiefly among the works of Spanish vihuelists who may have worked in Italy. After 1550 the changes in madrigal techniques are directed toward expressive writing, toward increasing the importance of one among several voices, and toward "concertato" madrigals. Some of the secular compositions by Giaches de Wert, Gesualdo, and Monteverdi are cases in point, for despite textual underlay in all parts there is some question as to how they are to be performed. They are seemingly constructed for rendition by a solo voice with the other four parts as accompaniment, but no specific directions are given. We know from many late 16th-century accounts that it was customary to sing one part as a solo and to use instruments or cembalo for the other parts.[1] The trend may also be seen in manuscripts such as the Bottegari Lutebook, which contains many beautiful and expressive solo songs composed during the last two decades of the century.

The new musical ideas were crystallized in the productions of a small group of Florentine gentlemen, literati, dilettantes and musicians—the *Camerata*—under the leadership of Count Bardi. They called their music *le nuove musiche,* the "new music"; their theorist was Vincenzo Galilei, but their ideas were exemplified in Peri's operas, *Dafne* and *Euridice,* and in the collection of songs Giulio Caccini published in 1601 under the title *Le nuove musiche.*

The idea of the solo song, or "monodia," as it was first called, as a vehicle for expressing highly emotional and pathetic sentiment, first manifested itself in Italy, but soon spread over all of Europe: into England, France, and, to a lesser extent, Spain. In Germany, where many of the composers were Italian-trained, the new expressive style took a curious turn; instead of being applied chiefly to secular music, it was reserved for the more important forms of sacred music: the motet, the cantata.

[1] See further discussion of this point under TO THE PERFORMER.

This can undoubtedly be attributed to Protestant, pietistic ideas then current that music should serve only the highest purposes, to praise God, and to elevate men's thoughts. Thus we find the most splendid examples of German solo song in devotional music, while secular songs remain the somewhat innocuous *Gesellschaftslieder* (social music), always slightly apart from the main stream of development of the art song.

*Monodia*—the term comes from the Camerata as a result of their investigations into ancient Greek music—originally meant a kind of sung poetic declamation in which the vocal line closely followed the inflections of spoken declamation and which should be governed almost solely by those inflections and verbal rhythm; in other words, a vocal line that was not primarily a melodic one conforming to rules of form and balance. The early monodies consequently contained a single emotional state set forth by the singer (melodically somewhat amorphous and rather static), accompanied by a single instrument—lute, theorbo, cembalo—with the meagerest sort of melodic and harmonic movement. We would call it today a "thin" accompaniment. This, of course, was intentional, for the Bardi group were certain that the Greeks declaimed their poetry thus, the music being subordinate to the words. On the other hand, the Camerata's concept of performance of music in the antique way led to the use of vocal ornaments, or *gorgia* (literally, "throat"), to heighten the effectiveness of the declamation, and the singers customarily improvised, or sometimes wrote out, runs, ornamental figures, trills, *groppi* (groups), *passaggi* (passages, or combinations of notes), the amount of ornamentation being dependent on the sentiments expressed in the text.[2]

The earliest forms of monody, those written by the Florentines Peri, Caccini, Rasi, Megli and others, are fairly simple and, in general, brief; the later ones, dating from around 1612 or 1615, became longer and more elaborate while still presenting a single idea or emotional state, with greater emphasis on the ornamentation and the virtuosity of the singer. These were often called "arie passeggiate."

The next stage in the development occurs about 1625, when we find brief passages of declamation on one or two notes being inserted in the monodies to serve as explanations, exclamations, or descriptions peripheral to the main theme of the work. Now the little songs assume a sectional character with distinct contrast between declamatory, or *recitando,* singing and a more melodic strain soon to be termed *aria* (air or melody). In 1625 Alessandro Grandi called such works "cantade," and this is thought to be the beginning of the use of the word "cantata."[3] Henceforth the sectional form rapidly replaced the earlier "monody," and by 1640 the latter term is no longer used. Instead we find "aria" (at this time meaning a strophic melody), "madrigal," or "cantata" used chiefly to denote secular song. At the same time came a greater formalism, with contrasts not only of a melodic nature but also of key and movement. The recitative became a longer, independent section, and a larger, more important form, the aria, evolved from the arioso. The cantata very quickly became the most important type of secular song, with a definite musical form consisting basically of contrasting sections such as aria—recitative—arioso—aria. The final development of the cantata is found in the works of Alessandro Scarlatti, of Hasse, and of Handel, where an extended plan, such as aria—recitative—aria—recitative—aria, or variants, is to be seen.

The *cantata a voce sola* with basso continuo is pure chamber music and may be said to be the vocal parallel to the violin sonata. Later cantatas, often called *concerti,* for one or more voices accompanied by strings or a small orchestra, somewhat lost the intimate character of the solo cantata and became more like small oratorios. They were frequently composed for special occasions such as royal birthdays, weddings, or national feast days.

The new style affected both secular and ecclesiastical music and resulted in an immense number of excellent songs for solo voice with instrumental accompaniment—cembalo, theorbo, chitarrone, viol, organ—music which, unfortunately, has been either forgotten or neglected. Much exists only in manuscript, some has been printed in such modern publications as the *Denkmäler der Tonkunst in Österreich,* the *Denkmäler deutscher Tonkunst,* Riemann's and Jeppesen's editions; little has found its way into the modern repertory. To exemplify this vast repertory, the selections in this volume have been chosen from secular and sacred songs, cantatas and motets. With a few exceptions, operas have been left aside

---

[2] Examples are the monodies of Peri, Rasi, Kapsberger, Saracini, Landi.

[3] For examples of early cantatas see the songs by Grandi, Strozzi and Rossi.

—not because they are either unworthy or uninteresting but because it is impossible to present a comprehensive and representative survey of them within the limits of this volume. Emphasis has been placed on composers significant in this florescence and important in their day, some of whom have become but names and whose works remain unknown.

Perhaps a word about the texts and their poetic background is in order. The period with which we are concerned saw the height of the development of the Baroque in Western Europe—in architecture, painting, literature, and music. The emphasis was upon intense emotionalism and exaggerated expressiveness, as is easily seen in the dome of S. Ignazio in Rome, for example, or Bernini's baldacchino in St. Peter's. The texts of the songs—sacred as well as secular—reflect this exaggeration; many are excellent examples of Italian *Marinismo,* French *préciosité,* Spanish *Gongorismo,* English *Euphuism,* all different names for very similar phenomena in the different countries, full of verbal tricks, of conceits, oxymora, farfetched metaphors and similes; many of them are exceedingly clever; some verses, on the other hand, are quite simple and very lovely; others are sardonic and humorous.

Another feature of the poetry which will undoubtedly strike the attention is the predominance of the pastoral atmosphere. Beginning in Italy as early as the late 15th century with Angelo Poliziano's *Orfeo* and Sannazaro's idyllic poetry, culminating in his *Arcadia* of 1504, it became the fashion to write about the simple, unsophisticated life of the mythical shepherds and shepherdesses whose lives and loves the writers felt were in such contrast with the artificial and sophisticated existences of the courts and cities of their own times. The pastoral movement was somewhat overshadowed early in the 16th century by the advent of *petrarchism*—that is, imitation of the form and emotional content of the poetry of Francesco Petrarca (1304–1474). This in turn waned slightly after the mid-century in favor of a renewed interest in, almost a passion for, the bucolic atmosphere. The poets imitated Virgil's *Bucolics* in such productions as Tasso's *Aminta* of 1573, Guarini's *Pastor fido* of the 1580s, Sidney's *Arcadia* of 1590—all immensely popular—and these were followed in Spain, Germany, England, and Italy by hosts of poets and versifiers who found the loves of Chloris, Phyllis, Amaryllis, Corydon *et al.* irresistibly attractive. The vogue endured for more than two hundred years, until well past the middle of the 18th century. It is a curious episode in literary history and a convention of interest to the scholar. The laments, the sufferings, the joys of the bucolic life are to be interpreted as applying to all humanity.

The manner of performance was an exact counterpart of the Baroque poetic style. The great singers of the period—Caccini, Peri, Vittoria Archilei, Rasi, La bell'Adriana, D'India, Barbara Strozzi—of whose art we have many descriptions, were often praised for their sensitive, eloquent interpretations of the true musical and literary meaning. The modern performer should try to execute these songs with the most careful regard for their emotional content and should keep in mind that they were truly *musica da camera,* performed for connoisseurs in most intimate surroundings. From various treatises on singing and on the art of embellishment such as those of Caccini, Bassano, Conforto, to mention only three of the important ones, we know a great deal about techniques of embellishment and improvisation as a means of heightening the expression and of demonstrating the virtuosity of the singer. The ornamentation, though following established precepts, was most often improvised, each singer having his characteristic style and technique, so it is of the greatest interest to find a number of songs with the embellishments included.[4] These might well be used as examples, if not for imitation, at least for study.

[4] In the present collection these are numbers 4, 5, 7, 9, 10, 11, 15, 16, 22, 34, 41, 46, 50.

# *To The Performer*

The successful performance of early music depends largely not only on a knowledge of the style of any given period but also of the manner in which the music might have been performed. By "manner" we mean the media used, the accepted types of ornamentation, the principles and concepts that governed expressive performance, tempo, dynamics, and the ideals of sound that prevailed. Some familiarity with a few of the most important ideas will materially aid the modern performer.

First, the exact manner of performance of the music seldom if ever is indicated on the printed page. The modern performer, expecting all information as to the composer's intentions—such as tempo and dynamic marking, directions for instruments or voices to be used—may be surprised and often baffled by compositions which specify none of these things. Music of past times could be performed in as great a variety of ways as suited the performers, the circumstances, and the taste of the times. A few examples from contemporary accounts of musical performances will make this clear.

In 1539, among the compositions performed for a princely wedding was what appears to be an *a cappella* piece, a four-voice madrigal with text underlay in all parts, which nonetheless was sung as a soprano solo accompanied by a harpsichord and an organ; another madrigal for the same festivity, this one in five parts, was sung by a single voice with four trombones playing the other parts.

From an account of 1565 we learn that a five-voice madrigal was sung by a soprano with four viols and additional accompaniment behind the scene consisting of a gamba and four trombones.

For the wedding festivities on the occasion of the marriage of the Grand Duke of Tuscany in 1589, several polyphonic pieces were sung as solos, accompanied by instruments: one by a large lute and two chitarroni (large lutes), another by a lute, chitarrone, and lira arciviolata (or lyra viol, a bowed instrument of intermediate size); still another by a large number of lyres, lutes, double harps, viols, gambas, trombones, and organ.

Michael Praetorius tells us in his *Syntagma musicum* (1619) that sacred motets for a chapel choir might be performed by the full choir as written, or by one or two solo voices with the organ using stops that have the effect of trombones. He also says that all parts may be played by various combinations of instruments without using voices at all.

The directions Heinrich Schütz gave for performing his *Historia der Auferstehung Jesu Christi* (Resurrection Story) (1623) include the following passage:

> When sometimes in the *Historia* only one person speaks, as for example the Lord Jesus, Mary Magdalene, etc. I have written a Duo. Here in special instances the personage of the Lord Christ can be sung with both voices, an Alto and a Tenor, or only one part sung and the other played on an instrument, or if desired it [the second part] may be omitted completely.

Clearly substitutes and allowances were often made! As late as 1748 J. J. Cassanéa de Mondonville advised his readers in *Pièces de clavecin avec voix ou violon* that persons who play the harpsichord and cannot sing may have the vocal part played by a violin. He says further that lacking both voice and violin the harpsichord accompaniment alone will suffice for the piece.

Instructions of this kind are many and demonstrate that no hard and fast rules as to medium were applied. To be sure, vocal polyphony could be performed unaccompanied if desired and any

XV

music could be played or sung as written. But in the extremely rare instances where a composer wanted his music performed only as written he gave specific directions, as did Alessandro Grandi in his 4th Sonata (1628) when he wrote "Sonata come sta" (Played as written). The numerous 17th-century collections marked "da cantare o sonare" (to sing or play) and the titles which advise that the violin can be replaced by a flute or a bass viol by a violin (!) testify to the great latitude allowed the performer.

Liberties taken with the length or overall form of compositions were also quite usual. Frescobaldi, the great Italian organist of the first quarter of the 17th century, printed in his volume of *Toccate* (1614) some suggestions for performance. One of his statements is that he has attempted "to plan the various sections so that they can be played independently of one another. The performer can stop wherever he wishes, and thus does not have to play them all."

Thus, most of the songs in this anthology could be perfectly well performed with accompaniment of some instrument other than harpsichord (for which the realizations here have been made.) A lute, piano, organ, viols—almost anything upon which harmonies can be played—would serve.

Second, the matter of ornamentation in all music of the Baroque period is extremely important. During the 16th and 17th centuries improvised ornaments, called *diminutions,* were customary. The term *diminution* may seem strange; but when one realizes that it refers to the breaking up of long note values—literally "diminishing" them into many short values—the logic is apparent. One may ask why a performer should add anything to a piece if the composer has already written it out, presumably as he wished it to be, and what might be the purpose of such ornamentation. The answer lies in a very ancient concept— the idea that it is good and legitimate to add something to enhance the music further. In his *Compendium musices* of 1552 Adrian Petit Coclico stresses this concept. Marc Pincherle sums up Coclico's thought as follows:

> The singer who does not sing the piece as it is written but also embellishes it, transforms, by means of the ornamentation, a simple, plain, ordinary, crude song into an elegant, ornamental song, a tasteless dish into a salted and seasoned viand (literally "meat with salt and mustard").[5]

Much later, in 1752, J. J. Quantz writes:

> If a solo is to do honour to its composer and to its performer . . . the performer must have an opportunity to demonstrate his judgment, inventiveness, and insight . . .[6]

So, in most of the music of the 16th, 17th, and most of the 18th centuries, the performer was expected to "grace" the melodic line, vocal or instrumental, thereby enhancing the work suitably and tastefully.

It is impossible to say exactly when the practice of diminution began, but as early as 1535, the first tutor appeared, Silvestro Ganassi's *Il Fontegara.* It was an instruction book primarily for recorder players, but equally applicable to other instrumentalists. It provided instruction in how to play the recorder and also in the art of making diminutions—to illustrate which Ganassi provided 175 examples of ornamented cadences. Other tutors for viols and for keyboard instruments soon followed; since this art was not exclusively instrumental, late in the century instruction books for the art of vocal diminution appeared. Example 1, from Giovanni Battista Bovicelli's *Regole Passaggi di musica* (1594), gives an idea of the style of vocal ornamentation for a rising stepwise passage. These tutors, of course, merely provided stereotyped models for the would-be virtuoso; the accomplished singer developed his own style and technique according to his "good taste and judgment." The words "good taste and judgment" are the clue to the application of such ornaments, and contemporary writers always stress the idea that such additions should be done in moderation and with "taste and judgment." *Diminutions* permitted singers to show not only their musical inventiveness but also their vocal

[5] *On the Rights of the Interpreter,* in the *Musical Quarterly* XLIV (1958), 156. Facs, ed. by Manfred Bukofzer: *Adrian Petit Coclico. Compendium musices, 1552.* Kassel, 1954.

[6] *On Playing the Flute,* ed. and transl. E. R. Reilly New York, 1966, VIII, 48.

*Example 1*

virtuosity, and it goes without saying that the practice was often abused.

With the advent of monody—an intimate vocal chamber music for connoisseurs and amateurs—new refined and elegant kinds of ornamentation were required, graces and accents that would increase the expressiveness of the rendition as well as enhance the vocal line. It must be kept in mind that the basic requirement was that the emotional content of the poem (the *affetto della parola*), the "passions", should be expressed as fully and artistically as possible. The oft-repeated words "passions," "conceit and humour of the words," "music capable of moving the passions of the mind" show that the singer was expected to give life to every nuance of the text. The embellishments necessary to "the good and true manner of singing . . . an art that admitteth no mediocrity . . . ," as Giulio Caccini put it, are explained in detail in the fore-

word to his *Nuove Musiche* (1602),[7] the first published collection of songs designed exclusively for solo voice.

The accents (*accenti*) and graces Caccini describes are the *trillo* (trill), *gruppo* (group), *cascata* (fall), *crescere e scemare della voce* (increasing and decreasing of the voice), *esclamazione* (exclamation), and *ribattuta di gola* (beating of the throat). For Caccini and the singers of most of the 17th century the *trillo* was executed on one note only; it should "begin with the first quarter note and beat every note with the throat upon the vowel 'a' to the final breve" (Ex. 2). The *gruppo* is performed on two notes and resembles the modern trill (Ex. 3). In Ex. 4 Caccini shows how both *gruppo* and *trillo* are written and performed. *Cascate* are ornamental running passages, usually over an octave (Ex. 5). *Ribattuta di gola* is an oscillation between two neighboring notes in a dotted rhythm that accelerates progressively and

[7] A translation of the Foreword to Giulio Caccini's *Le nuove musiche* [1602] may be found in Oliver Strunk, *Source Readings in Music History: The Baroque Era*, New York, 1965, pp. 17–32.

*Example 2*

*Example 3*

*Example 4*

*Example 5*

often leads into a trill (Ex. 6). *Crescere e scemare della voce* is a dynamic ornament also known as *messa di voce,* ———————— on one note. Caccini does not give an example, although he talks about it: "Exclamation is the principal means to move the affection, and exclamation properly is the decreasing of the voice and then increasing it more." It is a kind of reverse *messa di voce,* with a decrescendo followed by a crescendo. Caccini's description and example show clearly what he meant (Ex. 7).

Caccini also emphasizes a practice that is not exactly an ornament per se, but which he considered to be an important enhancement of the music. He calls this *sprezzatura*—"a certain noble neglect of the song" or a kind of "talking in harmony." From the examples he gives it is clear that he means *tempo rubato.*

The passionate, highly specialized style employed only for monody lasted some thirty years. By 1640 it had become passé and the new operatic and *bel canto* styles were beginning to take its place.

From that time onward ornaments, obligatory in all kinds of music, sacred as well as secular, became somewhat standardized. In some instances, especially in French songs, embellishments are indicated by symbols; more often such signs are lacking, leaving the addition of ornaments entirely to the performer's discretion. As to kinds of ornaments, their number is legion and the signs may differ from period to period, from country to country, and from composer to composer. How-

ever, the mordent, trill, appoggiatura, slide, acciaccatura and all the others are discussed again and again by writers of the period, many of whom provide explanatory tables in their published works showing exactly how each figure is to be performed. Thus it is relatively easy for the modern performer to determine the meaning of a symbol at any particular period. In addition, most of the ornaments together with their manner of execution have been discussed in various encyclopedias and dictionaries, in modern reprints and translations of 17th- and 18th-century works, and in modern books by Dolmetsch, Dannreuther, Donington, Harich, Schmitz and others. However, in applying ornaments to early music, two principles ought to guide the modern performer:

  a) Embellishments should be used only where they enhance, strengthen or emphasize expression of the text.
  b) Ornaments are almost always required at important cadences.

It is also important to keep in mind Thurston Dart's excellent advice:

> Ornaments are delicate, instinctive things; if they are not ornamental they are worse than useless, and anxiety about the right way to play [or sing] them must never be allowed to cloud a performer's sense of the underlying structure of the music they adorn.[8]

Ex. 8 presents a table of the most common ornaments in the 17th and 18th centuries. In addition to the above signs the French often use a simple + to indicate that an ornament is to be used, but the choice of ornament is left to the performer.

[8] Thurston Dart, *The Interpretation of Music,* New York, 1963, p. 102.

*Example 6*

*Example 7*

*Example 8*

The matter of tempo is another problem for to-day's performer. In early music, a kind of norm, or *tempo giusto* always existed; but the concept of this norm should not lead the performer to think that only one tempo was possible. Slower and faster tempos, appropriate to the style and character of the composition, were always used, the norm being merely a point of reference in determining the different speeds. The length of the motor unit, or quarter note, was originally understood to be equivalent to a man's leisurely stride or his regular pulse when breathing quietly. However, this standard of measurement was somewhat unsatisfactory, due to individual physiological differences. Seventeenth- and eighteenth-century writers, such as Mersenne, Simpson, Loulié, and Quantz, devoted much attention to the problem. Mersenne and Loulié each invented a pendulum-like apparatus to provide a means of measuring the duration of such a unit, but it was not until 1816, with Maelzel's metronome, that a reliable device for indicating tempo was perfected.

In general, for the earliest music the kind of note values used will give some indication of tempo.[9] If the basic movement of a piece is predominantly in quarters and eighths, the tempo will be moderate; if in eighths and sixteenths, the movement will be more lively; if in halves and quarters a slower, more grave tempo will prevail. The symbol c or O usually indicates a moderate tempo, especially if the quarter note is the unit. c or ¢ 2, O or O3 indicate a speed approximately double that of c and O.

Such marks do *not* indicate that the tempo is unvarying from beginning to end and we find in numerous early works clear statements that there

[9] In applying this rule-of-thumb, the performer should be warned that many older editions of early music were published without reduction of the old note values to modern equivalents. Everyone is familiar with 16th-century music printed in whole and half notes that give the impression of extremely slow tempos and are all too often rendered in lugubrious and funereal fashion. When performing from such editions, the editorial principles used should be consulted before deciding on a tempo.

are to be variations of tempo in any composition. Nicola Vicentino in 1555 says the singer should:

express those intonations accompanied by words with the proper passions—now joyful, now sad, sometimes sweet and sometimes harsh—and adhere to the pronunciation of the word and notes in his accents. Sometimes a certain manner of proceeding is used in the works that cannot be written down, as, to sing *piano* and *forte, presto* and *tardo,* and according to the words *move the tempo* to show the effects of the passions of the words and harmony . . . for the compositions sung with *mutations of the measure* is very welcome with such variety . . . rather than without variety right on to the end.[10] (Italics added)

Later Frescobaldi, too, says:

Do not keep strict time throughout but, as in modern madrigals, use here a slow tempo, there a fast one, and here one that, as it were, changes in the air, always in accordance with the expression and meaning of the words.[11]

Early in the 17th century "time words"—*tardo* (slow) and *presto* (fast)—begin to appear in Italian music, and by the end of the century a sizeable vocabulary is in current use. Sébastien de Brossard gives a very modern-looking list in his *Dictionnaire de musique* of 1703. Here are a few:

Largo — very slow, as if enlarging the measure and making the main beats often unequal, etc.

Adagio adagio — very slow.

Adagio — comfortably, *at your ease,* without pressing on, almost always slow and dragging the speed a little.

Lento — *slowly,* heavily, not at all lively or animated.

Andante — to stroll with even steps, means above all for Basso Continuos, that all the Notes must be made equal, and the Sounds well separated.

Allegretto — diminutive of Allegro, means *rather gaily,* but with a gracious, pretty, blithe gaiety.

Allegro — always Gay, and *decidedly lively;* very often quick and light; but also at times with a moderate speed, yet gay and lively.

Brossard's terms are generally valid for the early part of the 17th century.

In Quantz's *Essay on Playing the Flute* (1752) he not only gives time-words, but also works out a scheme for measuring tempo by the human pulse, which he estimates as averaging 80 beats per minute. He discusses the various tempos at length, but we may summarize his remarks in terms of M. M. markings as follows:

In common time ₵ —Allegro assai    ♩ = 80
                 Allegretto       ♩ = 80
                 Adagio cantabile ♪ = 80
                 Adagio assai     ♪ = 80

In *alla breve* ₵ —Allegro assai    o = 80
                 Allegretto       ♩ = 80
                 Adagio cantabile ♩ = 80
                 Adagio assai     ♪ = 80

Quantz did not expect these tempos to be taken as absolute, for he says also that:

it is most important to consider both the word indicating the tempo at the beginning of the piece and the fastest note used in the passage-work.

He says further:

I do not pretend that a whole piece should be measured off in accordance with the pulse beat; this would be absurd and impossible. My aim is simply to show how in at least two, four, six, or eight pulse beats, any tempo you wish can be established, and how you can achieve a knowledge of the various categories of tempo by yourself that will lead you to further inquiry. After some practice an idea of [each] tempo will gradually so impress itself upon your mind that it will no longer be found necessary always to consult the pulse beat.[12]

During the 17th century two distinct schools of interpretation developed: the Italian and the French. Curiously, the German and English composers developed no distinctive style of their own but adopted the Italian and the French, often priding themselves (as Telemann did) on being able to compose in either. While the embellishments were basically the same in both schools, the manner in which they were employed differed. The Italian style was said to be "fiery"—full of

---

[10] Nicola Vicentino, *L'antica musica ridotta alla moderna prattica,* Lib. 4°, p. 54.

[11] Girolamo Frescobaldi, *Toccate . . . e partite d'intavolatura,* 1614.

[12] Quantz, *op. cit.,* VII, vii, 48.

runs and *passaggi,* characterized generally by an energetic rhythm. Also, very often all the embellishments were written out. The French style, on the other hand, largely as a result of Lully's style and influence, was more elegant and restrained, the smaller graces—*pincés* (mordents), *coulés* (slurs), *tremblements* (trills)—being preferred to the brilliant runs and roulades of the Italians. The distinction between the two styles was generally recognized and often passionately discussed, with sides being taken as to which style was better. François Raguenet, in his *Comparison between the French and Italian Music* (1702) says:

> The French, in their airs, aim at the soft, the easy, the flowing and coherent; . . . The Italians venture at everything that is harsh and out of the way, but then they do it like people that have a right to venture and are sure of success . . . as the Italians are naturally much more brisk than the French, so are they more sensible of the passions and consequently express'em more lively in all their productions.[13]

And Quantz says:

> Italian music is less circumscribed than any other, while the French is almost too much so, . . . Yet the manner of *playing* of the French is not to be scorned; on the contrary, the beginner is to be advised to use French propriety and clarity to temper the obscurity of the *playing* of the Italians . . .[14]

A fairly reliable clue to the style of a piece may be obtained from the language of the tempo and expression marks, as Thurston Dart suggests.[15] The presence of such terms as *vite, lentement, doux, gaiement,* would indicate that the idiom is French, whereas words such as *allegro, grave, lento, adagio* would imply the Italian style.

Performance of the accompaniment also requires knowledge of the style of the period. For the earliest songs and monody (the pieces by Peri, Caccini, D'India, Rasi, Monteverdi) the bass line and its harmonies may be played on any chordal instrument or combination of instruments, though care should be taken not to make the accompaniment too thick. The monodists designed their music for a minimal number of accompanying instruments—often only a chitarrone or large lute[16]—so the texture should be rather thin and the sonority light.

In songs written after the first third of the century, the basso continuo—thorough-bass, figured or unfigured—became the customary accompaniment. This was usually played on a harpsichord (or occasionally an organ, if a sacred work) together with a continuo instrument to double the bass line. The added instrument was most often a viol da gamba, later a cello or violone, or both, but the bassoon was also much used in instrumental ensembles. The doubling of the bass line was necessary because the sound of the harpsichord dies away very quickly and an instrument which could sustain the melodic bass added greatly to the firmness of the foundation over which the harmonies are erected.

Throughout the Baroque period the basso continuo accompaniment was always improvised from the bass. This improvisation was a real art, and good continuo players were highly esteemed. Because the accompaniment is improvisatory in nature, the figures being nothing more than indications of the harmony, it is extremely important that the realization be fluid, somewhat transparent, and above all avoid "a relentless succession of four-note chords" which provide full harmony and little else. What is wanted in a good continuo player is a sense of style and of the spirit of the piece. Quantz says that even though a player may have an exhaustive knowledge of thorough-bass, he may nevertheless be only a poor accompanist. He gives some advice in this regard which modern continuo players would do well to heed:

> The general rule of thorough-bass is that you always play in four parts; yet if you wish to accompany well, a better effect is often produced if you do not bind yourself very strictly to this rule, and if you leave out some parts, or even double the bass an octave higher with the right hand. For just as a composer is neither able nor compelled to set a three-, four-, or five-part instrumental accompaniment to all melodies, so not every melody allows an accompaniment of full chords upon the keyboard; hence an accompanist must govern himself more by the individual case than by the general rules of thorough-bass.[17]

Francesco Geminiani, too, remarked upon the duties of the accompanist in his *Rules for Playing in*

---

[13] The J. E. Galliard translation (1709) edited by Oliver Strunk: *Source Readings in Music History, The Baroque Era,* pp. 117–18.
[14] Quantz, *op. cit.,* ch. X, no. 19.
[15] Dart, *op. cit.,* p. 94.

[16] Peri's opera *Euridice* had for instrumental accompaniment only a cembalo, theorbo, lira grande, and lute.
[17] Quantz, *op. cit.,* VII, vi, 4.

*a True Taste:*

> With respect to the thorough-bass on the Harpsichord . . . (I) have given the following short rules, for the use of those who desire to accompany in a good Taste. They must be sure to place the chords between the hands, in such a manner as to produce (by passing from one chord to another) at once both an agreeable Harmony and Melody. Sometimes playing many chords, and at other times few, for our delight arises from the variety. Whenever the upper part stops, and the Bass continues, he who accompanies must make some melodious variation on the same harmony, in order to awaken the imagination of the performer, whether he sings or plays, and at the same time to give pleasure to the hearer . . . In accompanying grave movements, he should make use of the *Acciacature,* for these rightly placed, have a wonderful effect; and now and then should touch the several notes of the chord lightly one after another, to keep the harmony alive. In swift movements the left hand must strike the plain note of the Bass, and the right [hand] the chords in such a manner as not to cause a confusion of sounds, else it will be most prudent to leave out the chords . . . he who has no other qualities than that of playing the notes in time, and placing the figures, as well as he can, is but a wretched Accompanyer.[18]

Many other such statements could be adduced; instead we may here summarize three general principles emphasized by all writers on the art of accompanying:

1) The accompaniment should support and enhance but never overshadow the solo part.

2) The left hand in general is to play the bass line alone; the right hand is to play the chords necessary to fill out the accompaniment. (To be sure, "extended chords" divided between the hands are used, as recommended by Neidt, C. P. E. Bach and others, but in the main the left hand is supposed to be free to deal with the evolving figurations

3) The accompaniment for the most part should stay below the vocal line. (This is not always possible, especially in songs for bass, where vocal line and basso continuo may be essentially the same.)

Clearly a thick or heavy accompaniment was not what was wanted; rather a tasteful, well-executed improvisation suited to the style of the piece was the *desideratum.* In the 17th and 18th centuries the continuo was looked upon as the "foundation of the building," as Couperin said, which, even though it may scarcely be noticed, nevertheless supports the whole structure. It is indispensable in the performance of baroque music.

> . . . the emptiness of a performance without this accompanying instrument is, unfortunately, made apparent to us far too often . . . No piece can be well performed without some form of keyboard accompaniment. Even in heavily scored works, such as operas performed out of doors, where no one would think that the harpsichord could be heard, its absence can certainly be felt.[19]

Musical notation does not always suggest the way the music is to be played, therefore the harpsichordist will do well to observe certain well-known Baroque practices. In playing chords of more than two or three notes it is advisable to "spread" them ever so slightly—not as much as an arpeggio would require but sufficiently to make the notes sound very rapidly in succession. This builds sonority and avoids the harshness that occurs from simultaneous sounding of the high harmonics.

Also it is advisable to hold down as many notes in the same harmony as possible when there is movement among the chord members. Rameau advises this in his *Pièces de Clavessin* (1724) (see Ex. 9).

Arpeggiation of chords in very slow movement is always good, even though there may be no specific indication. Frescobaldi recommends this practice in the following words:

[18] Francesco Geminiani, *Rules for Playing in a True Taste, on the Violin German Flute Violoncello and Harpsichord particularly the Thorough Bass,* Opera VIIII, (ca. 1745), p. 2.

[19] C. P. E. Bach, *Essay on the True Art of Playing Keyboard Instruments,* pp. 172–73.

*Example 9*

The beginnings of the toaccatas should be somewhat adagio and arpeggiando; likewise, in the syncopations or dissonances, even in the middle of the work, they will be played by both hands (i.e. arpeggiated) so that the instrument will not sound hollow; and these *batteries* may be used at the discretion of the player.[20]

Example 10, given in Thomas Mace's *Musick's Monument* (1676), shows a rather surprising but entirely legitimate way of arpeggiating chords.

As for techniques of playing expressively, Couperin's remarks in *L'Art de toucher le clavecin* (1717) are valuable and applicable generally:

> . . . the harpsichord can be made to sound expressive by means of the *aspiration* and the *suspension*. The *suspension*—a note played late—corresponds to a crescendo on a stringed instrument, and is scarcely used except in slow and tender pieces. The *aspiration*—a note quitted early—corresponds to a diminuendo, and it should be less abrupt in a slow piece than in a quick one. The long mordent on the harpsichord corresponds to a vibrato on a bowed instrument [The vibrato at that time was an ornament, not a technique.] Appoggiaturas of every kind must be struck on the beat, not before it . . . Shakes must always begin on the upper note, and they must grow faster towards the end . . . Slow pieces should be played a little faster on the harpsichord than they would on other instruments . . .[21]

Two further points essential to proper performance of Baroque music are the practices of overdotting and inequality. Dotted rhythms should always have the difference between the lengths of the notes emphasized to sharpen the rhythm. Thus a dotted eighth and sixteenth will be played as if the eighth had another dot and the sixteenth as if it were a thirty-second. This is never written out—it is simply understood that the first note is

lengthened and the second made very short.

Inequality is a somewhat different matter, and is essential in French style. Couperin says "The Italians write their music in its true time-values, but we do not. They play a diatonic succession of quarter notes evenly, whereas we always make the first of each pair a little longer than the second. This inequality should be more pronounced in a gay piece than in a sad one." [22] There are, however, certain places where inequality must not be used: when dots are over all notes it means they are to be played perfectly evenly, and when there is a slur and dot over each pair it means that the second note is to be held longer than the first. Inequality is not used in rapid passages or when there are repeated or disjunct notes, or when more than two notes are slurred together. Often the words *notes égales* or *mesurés* appear; these also mean the notes are to be played evenly.

The harpsichord was unquestionably preferred to the piano until about 1770, after which time the latter gradually superseded the former. It may be taken as a rule, therefore, that the harpsichord is the proper instrument to use for music written before 1770, the piano for music written after 1790. This does not mean that the pieces in this volume cannot be played on the piano; they can indeed, but the heavier sonority and markedly different sound of the piano alters—sometimes radically—the effect that would be given by the harpsichord. It would be absurd and unrealistic to suggest that performance of this music should be confined to use of the original instruments. We may ask however with Thurston Dart that

> the keyboard player, no matter what his instrument, should do all he can to meet an early composer on his own ground by discovering the lines along which he thought and the way in which he planned and played his music; for there is no other way of bridging the broken years between "then" and "now" [23]

[20] Frescobaldi, *op. cit.*, Lib. I°, 1637, p. 1.

[21] The translation and paraphrasing of Couperin's intentions may be found in Dart, *Op. cit.*, p. 80. The original may be found on pp. 16, 17, 18, 22, 23, 24, and 42 of *L'Art de toucher le clavecin* Paris, 1714.

[22] *Ibid.*, p. 38 of the Couperin.

[23] Dart, *Op. cit.*, p. 76.

*Example 10*

as interpreted by Mace

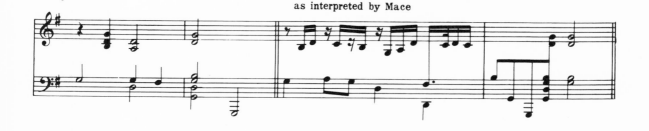

# *Editorial Principles*

The transcriptions have been made as accurate and faithful as possible. Note values in general remain unchanged from those of the original. Where reductions have been made, corresponding values are shown at the beginning of the piece. It should be noted that in a number of instances a section in triple rhythm (3/2) has been left in longer note values, 𝅝 and 𝅗𝅥 . This kind of notation always implies a *proportion,* the notes of each measure in triple meter to be sung in the same amount of time required for the two or four of the preceding duple meter; thus it indicates a faster movement.

Clefs, unless shown to be otherwise at the beginning of a piece, are to be understood as being those of the original.

Accidentals are modernized in the score whenever there is a likelihood of confusion, e.g. B♯ is always changed to the modern B♮. Figured basses are given as in the originals; the player must therefore understand that in early thoroughbass, the ♮ is rarely used; the ♭ indicates a lowering of a tone, or a minor third, the ♯ a raising of a tone, or a major third. Thus, in the key of E♭, a C on the bass with a ♯ below would indicate c, e♮, g. Editorial accidentals are shown above the staff. Suggested tempo markings and any other editorial additions are enclosed in square brackets.

Obvious errors in the original (misplaced accidentals, dots lacking, missing flags or stems, incomplete signatures, etc.) have been corrected without comment. Any correction or alteration of the musical text is explained in a footnote. Spelling of the texts has been for the most part changed to conform with modern usage.

In the case of lute songs, the lute part has simply been transcribed as it stands, with no additions or omissions, nor has any attempt been made to alter the free-voiced character of the accompanying part. The nature and limitations of the lute often cause a very transparent accompaniment, with incomplete chords and weak sonority, although a full harmony is implied. In playing these on the harpsichord or piano, the accompanist would be justified in supplying a missing harmony note or two, but such have not been added to our transcriptions.

In the case of the songs with basso continuo, the editor has tried to avoid the common error of providing too thick or heavy an accompaniment. Therefore every effort has been made to realize the accompaniment rather simply in the style of the period, according to the sound of the instruments then in use, and to avoid modern harmonies. The original bass lines and figures, which are given in each instance, have been scrupulously observed with no changes. In realizing the basses the editor has tried to adhere to the rules laid down by 17th- and 18th-century theorists.[24] In most cases the realization was conceived for harspichord rather than for pianoforte.

Time signatures are generally left as in the originals. During the 17th and 18th centuries ¢ was the usual symbol for 4/4 and had no connotation of a faster tempo. There has been no attempt to solve the very difficult problem of tempos. The editorial tempo indications are to be taken for what they are intended to be, merely suggested tempos and for the most part subjective. Sixteenth- and seventeenth-century composers rarely indicate speed or dynamics, leaving it to the taste and discretion of the performer whether he should sing loud or soft, fast or slow. Therefore no dy-

[24] The reader is referred to F. T. Arnold's excellent and indispensable work *The Art of Accompaniment from a Thorough-Bass as practised in the XVIIth & XVIIIth Centuries* (repr. ed. New York, Dover Publications, Inc. 1965) for more detailed information on this subject.

namic markings or ornaments are given except when the composer himself has indicated them, since the dynamics are determined by the text, and the music is intended to be the interpretation of the feeling expressed by the poet. The essential thing for the singer is to understand the text thoroughly by careful study of the poetry. Without this he cannot hope to render the music effectively and authoritatively. The translations provided are intended to convey accurately the sense of the verses and should not be used for singing. They are rather in the nature of close paraphrases than exact word-for-word renderings. No attempt has been made to put them into verse or even poetic style.

It is the editor's hope that acquaintance with these enchanting songs will afford pleasure to the user as well as an insight into musical practice of a former time, and that they will provide additions to the repertory of solo singers and source material for the historian.

*Carol MacClintock*

# Selected Bibliography of Works on Performance Practice

Bach, C. P. E., *Essay on the True Art of Playing Keyboard Instruments,* ed. and transl. W. J. Mitchell, New York, 1949.

Couperin, François, *L'Art de toucher le clavecin,* Paris, 1717.          ed. A. Linde, English transl. by M. Roberts, Wiesbaden, 1933.

Dannreuther, Edward, *Musical Ornamentation,* 2 vols, London, [1893–95].

Dart, Thurston, *The Interpretation of Music,* London, 1954.

Dolmetsch, Arnold, *The Interpretation of the Music of the XVIIth and XVIIIth Centuries Revealed by Contemporary Evidence,* rev. ed., London, 1946.

Donington, Robert, *The Interpretation of Early Music,* 3rd ed., New York, 1965.

Ferand Ernest T., *Improvisation in Nine Centuries of Western Music,* Vol. XII in *Anthology of Music,* Cologne, 1961.

*Grove's Dictionary of Music and Musicians,* 5th ed., ed. E. Blom. Articles on *Ornamentation* and *Ornaments,* Vol. VI, pp. 365–448.

Pincherle, Marc, *On the Rights of the Interpreter in the Performance of 17th- and 18th-century Music* in *Musical Quarterly,* XLIV (1958), 144–66.

Quantz, Johann Joachim, *On Playing the Flute,* ed. and transl. Edward R. Reilly, New York, 1966.

Raguenet, François, *A Comparison between the French and Italian Musick,* transl. from the French by J. E. Galliard (1709); ed. Oliver Strunk in *Musical Quarterly,* XXXII (1946), 411–36. Also available under the original title *Parallèle des Italiens et des Francais* in *Source Readings in Music History,* selected and annotated by Oliver Strunk: The Baroque Era, New York, 1965, pp. 113–28.

Tosi, Pier Francesco, *Opinioni de' cantori antichi e moderni . . . ,* Bologna, 1723. Transl. by J. E. Galliard as *Observations on the Florid Song,* London, 1743. Reprinted, London, 1926.

# PART I

# Songs by Italian Composers

## 1 · ANONYMOUS,

*Occhi de l'alma mia*

1. Oc - chi, oc - chi dell' al - ma mia, vi - va - ci e so - li, Deh, s'io ar - do per voi den - tro e di fuo - ra, La - scia - te ch'io vi ba - ci, la - scia - te ch'io vi ba - ci, an -

-che ch'io mo - - ra, an - che ch'io mo - ra.

Occhi, occhi dell' alma mia, vivaci e soli,
Deh, s'io ardo per voi dentro e di fuora,
Lasciate ch'io vi baci, anche ch'io mora.

Occhi vivi d'amor fiammelli ardenti,
Deh, se un lungo servir merta mercede,
Mirate se n' è degna la mia fede.

Occhi, sì dolc' è il ben che si desia
Del amato tesor' quando si more,
Deh! spargetene un poco entro al mio core.

Occhi, se per pietà non che per mio merto,
Non impetro da voi qualche conforto;
Voi, dolchi occhi, voi mi avete morto.

Eyes of my beloved, flashing and unique, since I long for you within me and without, let me kiss you, even if I die for it.

Eyes that flash the burning flames of love, if long servitude deserves a reward, see if my fidelity is worthy of it.

O Eyes! the pleasure one desires from the beloved object when one is about to die is so sweet! Please, sprinkle a little of it in my heart.

Eyes, unless through pity rather than because I desire it, you do not give me some comfort, you will be the cause of my death.

## 2 · COSIMO BOTTEGARI (1554–1620),

*Aria da cantar stanze*

Non è pena maggior, cortesi Amanti
Voi che donasti a duo' begl' occh'il core,
Che quando l'uomo alla sua Donna innanti
Far palese non poss' il suo dolore,
E quantunqu'ella il cor vegg' ai sembianti
Non si muov' à pietà di chi si more:
Gran miseria 'l suo amor tener' celato
E, amand' altrui, non esser punto amato.

There is no greater pain, courtly lovers,
You who may have given your hearts to two
beautiful eyes, than when, before his Lady, a man
cannot make known his anguish, and when she,
seeing the state of his heart, is not moved to pity
by him who is dying;
Great misery it is to keep one's love hidden and,
loving another, not to be loved at all.

## 3 · BOTTEGARI,

*Morte da me*

Mor - te,_____ da me tant'a - spet - ta - ta, vie - ni: E

fa che ven - ga si se - cre - ta e len - ta, Che'l

tuo ve - nir il mio_____ mo - rir non_____ sen - ta.

O vien! con quel - la_____ fret - ta co - me da ciel sa - et - ta, co - me da

Morte, da me tant' aspettata, vieni:
E fa che venga si secreto e lenta,
Che'l tuo venir il mio morir non senta.
O vien! con quella fretta
Come dal ciel saetta,
Che tuona e lampa e fulmina in un punto.
Così 'l mio core sia da te disgiunto.

*B. Castiglione*

Oh Death, so long awaited, come! and may your
coming be so silent and so slow that as I die
I will not perceive your arrival.
Oh come—as swiftly as lightning
darts from the sky, thundering and flashing,
destroying everything at one blow!
So may my heart be separated from me by you.

## 4 · LEONORA ORSINA (fl. 1560–1580),

*Per pianto la mia carne*

| | |
|---|---|
| Per pianto la mia carne si distilla | My flesh melts away in tears as |
| Si com' al sol la neve, | snow does beneath the sun, or as |
| O com' al vento si disfa la nebbia; | the cloud clears away before the |
| Non so che farmi debbia. | wind; I know not what to do. Just |
| Or pensat' al mio mal qual esser deve. | think how great must be my pain! |

## 5 · HIPPOLITO TROMBONCINO (fl. 1575–1620),

*Io son ferito*

Io son fe - ri - to, ahi las - so,

ahi, las - - - so, e chi mi die - de Ac -

- cu-sar pur vor - rei, ac - cu-sar pur vor - rei, ma non

ho ____ pro va;  Nè  senz'___  in - di - zio al mal____

____ non si da fe - de,  Nè get - ta san - gue la mia

pia - ga nuo - - - va.  Io  spem' e mo -

- - - ro,  io spem' e mo - ro;  il

col - po non si ve - de, La mia ne - mi - c'ar - ma - - ta non

si ___ tro - va.    Che sia ___    tor - nat' a

le - i,    cru - del par - ti - to, Che sol m'ab-bia a sa -

-nar chi m'ha fe - ri - - to.    Che sol m'ab-bia a sa - nar ___

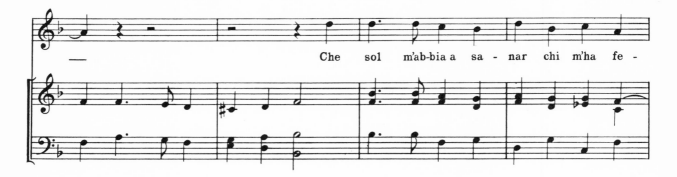

Io son ferito, ahi lasso, e chi mi diede
Accusar pur vorrei, ma non ho prova;
Nè senz' indizio al mal non si da fede,
Nè getta sangue la mia piaga nuova.
Io spem' e moro; il colpo non si vede,
La mia nemica armata non si trova.
Che sia tornat' a lei, crudel partito,
Che sol m'abbia a sanar chi m'ha ferito.

I am smitten, woe is me! and I want to accuse the
one who wounded me but I have no proof; and
people do not believe in a wrong when there is no
evidence, and my strange wound sheds no blood!
I suffer and die. The wound cannot be seen and
my well-armed foe cannot be found. What a cruel
fate, that only she can cure me who dealt me the
wound!

6 · JACOPO PERI  (1561–1633),

*Tu dormi*

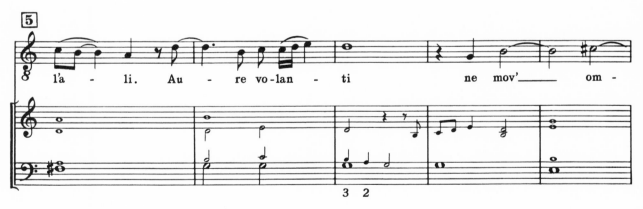

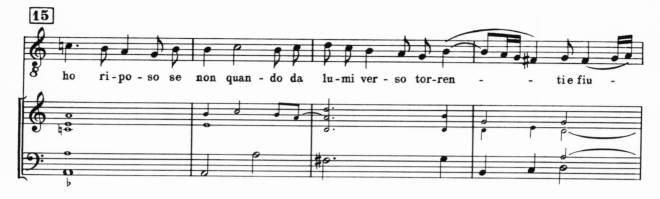

ho ri-po-so se non quan-do da  lu-mi ver-so tor-ren — — tie fiu —

-mi, esc' al not-tur-no sol,  à——— me——— gio - io - so.

Tu  lo splen-dor degl' ar-gen-ta-ti rai  non  ri - mi -

-ri,  e tu sta-i  sord' al duol'——— che m'ac-co - ra;  io

sent' e veg-gio ogn'or_____ l'au - ra e l'au-ro - ra.

11 #10

**35** [2ª parte]

Tu dor - mi, e non a-scol - ti me che pre - go e so-

**40**

-spi - ro, e pian-go, e bra - mo e nell' al - to si-

6                4    #

**45**

-len -tio o - ra ti chia - mo.                Ben

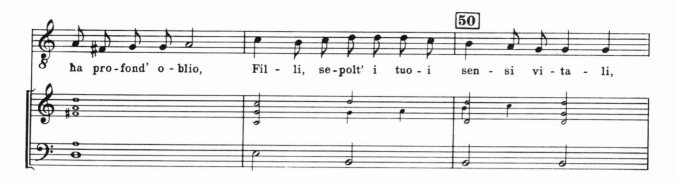

ha pro-fond' o-blio,     Fil - li, se-polt' i tuo - i     sen-si vi-ta - li,

e prov'_____ in ____ va - no     de - star in te pie-tad, d'al -

- -ma che mo - re.          Non è Fe - bo lon - ta - no;

vien l'al - ba ru-gia-do - sa;____          Ma che, dorm' e ri -

-po-sa,___ Non piang' in-dar-no i suoi tor-men-ti___ il co - re;

e se non sen - ti tu, e se non sen - ti tu,

mi sent'___ a - mo - re, mi sent'___ a - mo - re.

Tu dor - mi, ed i - o pur pian - go, O Fil - li, O___

del mio cor dol - ce tor - men - to,        e co'l mio pian - to io mir il Ciel' in-

-ten - to.        En-tro piu - me d'o - do-ri tu ri-pos' il bel fian-co;        io, __

__ fra mil - le do-lo - ri        sen - to sen-za pie-tà ve-nir-

- mi man-co.        O son - no,        o tu che por - ti pa-ce ai

Tu dormi, e'l dolce sonno ti lusinga con l'ali.
Aure volanti ne mov' ombra giamai, taci li pianti.
Io, che non ho riposo
se non quando da lumi verso torrent' e fiumi,
esc' al notturno sol, à me gioioso.
Tu lo splendor degl' argentati rai
non rimiri, e tu stai
sord' al duol che m'accora;
io sent' e veggio ogn' or l'aura e l'aurora.

Tu dormi, e non ascolti me che prego e sospiro
e piango e bramo, e nell' alto silentio ora ti
    chiamo;
Ben ha profond' oblio, o Filli, sepolt' i tuoi sensi
    vitali,
e prov' in vano destar in te pietad', alma che
    more.
Non è Febo lontano, vien l'alba rugiadosa;
Ma che, dorm' e risposa,
Non piang' indarno i suoi tormenti il core;
e se non senti tu, mi sent' amore.

Tu dormi, ed io pur piango, o Filli, o del mio cor
    dolce tormento,
e cò 'l mio pianto io mir' il Cielo intento.
Entro piume d'odori tu ripos' il bel fianco;
io fra mille dolori sento senza pietà venirmi
    manco.
O sonno, o tu che porti pace ai cori e le menti
    egri conforti,
Ti non chiamo giamai; ma sol desio
che nei sospir' aquet' il morir mio.

You are sleeping and sweet slumber caresses you with his wings. Neither passing breezes nor shadows move; trees are still. I, who have no rest except when I weep torrents and floods, go out under the night sky, joyous to me. You do not see the splendor of the moon's silvery rays and you remain deaf to the sorrow which disheartens me; I see always the dawn and feel the breeze.

You are sleeping and you do not hear me praying and sighing; and I weep and suffer from desire and call upon you in the deep silence. Your forgetfulness is profound, o Phyllis; your perceptions are buried; in vain the dying soul tries to awaken pity in you. Phoebus is not far away, the rosy dawn is coming. But you sleep and rest; your heart does not weep in vain for its torments. And if you feel nothing, I feel myself suffering from love.

You are sleeping; meanwhile I weep, o Phyllis, o sweet torment of my heart; and as I weep I look to Heaven intently. In perfumed down your lovely form reposes; in a thousand dolors, pitilessly, I feel myself swooning. Oh Sleep, thou who bringest peace to hearts and comfort to sick souls, I no longer call upon you; my only desire is that my complaints shall be calmed by death.

## 7 · GIULIO CACCINI (1545–1618),

*Sfogava con le stelle*

-te, Men-tre co-sì splen-de - te la sua ra - - ra bel - ta - te, Co-sì mo-stra-te à

le - i, Men-tre con-tan-to ar-de - te I__ vi - vi ar-do - - - ri

mie - i.    La fa-re-ste col vo-stro au-reo sem-bian-te Pie-to-sa, sì,    pie-

11  ×10 11 14

-to - sa sì    co - me me fa - te a-man - te.    La fa-re-ste col

6        6      11 #10 14

vo-stro au-reo sem-bian-te Pie-to-sa, sì, pie-to-sa sì co-me me fa-

-te a - man - te, Co - me me fa - - - - -

- - - - te a - man - te.

Sfogava con le stelle un' infermo d'amore
Sotto notturno cielo il suo dolore;
E dicea fisso in loro,
O immagini belle del Idol mio ch'adoro,
Sì come a me mostrate
mentre così splendete
la sua rara beltate,
Così mostrate à lei
mentre cotanto ardete
i vivi ardori miei;
La fareste col vostro aureo sembiante
Pietosa, sì come me ne fata amante.

*O. Rinuccini*

There appeared under the stars a man sick with love, and under the night sky he disclosed his pain; and he said, his eyes fixed on them, "Oh, lovely images of my adored Idol, just as you show me her rare beauty as you shine so brightly, in the same way show her my keen pangs. Perhaps you might make her pitiful with your golden aspect, just as you made me loving.

## 8 · CACCINI,

*Ohimè, se tant' amato*

[Not fast; expressively]

Ohi - mè,  Ohi - mè,  se tant' a - ma-te di sen-tir dir "Ohi - mè;"

Deh, _____ Deh, per-chè fa - te chi di-ce "ohi-mè" mo-ri - re, chi di-ce "ohi-mè" mo-ri-

-re, chi di-ce "ohi-mè" mo - ri - re?  S'io mo - ro,

un sol po-tre-te lan - gui - do e do-lo-ros' "ohi-mè" sen-ti - re;  Ma

se, cor mio, vor-re - te che vit' abb' io da voi che vit' abb' io da voi, e voi da

me, e voi da me, e_____ voi da me, a - vre-te mil-le dol - ce "ohi - mè," a -

-vre-te mil-le dol - ce "ohi - mè," a - vre-te mil-le dol - ce "ohi - mè."

Ohimè, se tant' amate
di sentir dir "ohimè",
Deh, perchè fate che dice ohimè morire?
S'io moro, un sol potrete
e doloroso ohime sentire;
Ma se, cor mio, vorrete
che vit' abb' io da voi,
e voi da me avrete mille dolci "ohimè."

Alas, if you are so fond of hearing
someone say "alas," woe is me;
why do you slay the man who says "alas?"
If I die you will hear only one sad "alas,"
but if, my heart, you want me to continue
to live because of you,
you can receive a thousand sweet "alas"
from me.

## 9 · FRANCESCO RASI   (fl. 1590–1625),

*Indarno Febo*

* Barring as in original

E tra bell' er - be di ru-scell' il suo -

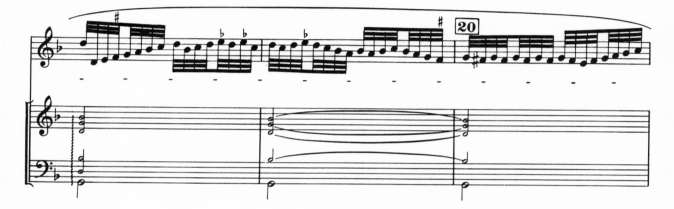

- - - - no; Ch'io lon-ta - no da voi nul - la non

sen - to. Oi - mè, oi - mè, dell' es-ser mi - o po-co ra-

-gio - no:    ch'io lon - ta - no da  voi    nul - - la non so - no.

Indarno Febo il suo bel oro eterno,
E Cinthia mi disvela il puro argento,
Ch'io lontano da voi nulla non scerno.

E mov' indarno lusinghevol vento,
E tra bell'erbe di ruscell' il suono;
Ch'io lontano da voi nulla non sento.

Oimè, dell'esser mio poco ragiono:
Ch'io lontano da voi nulla non sono.
                                    G. Chiabrera

Though Phoebus unveils for me his lovely
eternal gold, and Cynthia her pure silver,
I see nothing when I am far away from you.

Though gentle breezes blow, and the rivulet
murmurs in the grasses, I hear nothing when
I am far away from you.

Alas, I speak little about myself, for
I am nothing when I am away from you.

## 10 · RASI,

*Ahi, fuggitivo ben*

Ahi,— ahi,— fu-gi-ti-vo ben co — me si—

to — sto, Scon-so-la — ti la-scia-sti i miei de — si -

-ri. Deh,— co-me sia ch'a miei do - lo - ri a-co - sto,

Di vi-ver lie - ta____ più,__las - sa de-si - ri? O____

(III)

val - li, O____ fiu - mi,        O____        O pog - gi, O pog - gi,

"O," tu ri-po-sta,        Dol - ce____ lo-co pie-to-so a' miei so - spi -

- ri.  Se rim-bom - ba-sti a' miei gra - - vi ac -

(IV)

-cen - ti, U - dit', or pre - go, u - dit', or pre-

-go, i du - ri,_____ i du - ri miei la - men - ti.

Ahi, fuggitivo ben come si tosto
Sconsolati lasciasti i miei desiri.
Deh, come sia ch'a' miei dolori acosto,
Di viver lieta più, lassa, desiri?
O valli, o fiumi, o poggi—"O" tu riposti,
Dolce loco pietoso a' miei sospiri.
Se rimbombasti ai miei gravi accenti,
Udit', or prego, i duri miei lamenti.

*Fr. Rasi*

Alas, my lost love! How soon you left all my desires unsatisfied! How can it be that when you see my anguish you can desire to live happily? Ah, valleys, hills, rivers, glades; lovely scenes which had pity on my sorrows! If once you echoed to my joyous accents, hearken now to my bitter lamenting!

### 11 · JOHANN HIERONYMO KAPSBERGER (c. 1575–1661),

*Interrotte speranze*

[Con affetto; poco recitando]

In - ter-rot - te spe-ran - ze,__ e fer - ma fe - de, fiam -

Chitarrone

-me e stra - li pos-sen - ti in de - bil co - re, Nu -

-drir__ sol di so - spir un fer' ar - - - do - re, e ce -

-lar    il tuo  mal qual al  -  tri  il ve  -  de.

RITORNELLO

Se - guir di va - go e fug - gi - ti - vo pie - de  l'or  -  me ri-

-vol - te a vo - lun - ta - rio er - ro  -  re;  Per - der del se - me spars' e'l

der la-gri - man    -    do i lu - stri in - tie - ri.

*RITORNELLO*

Orig. Tablature

Que - sti ch'à voi qua - si gran fa - sci in-vio, Don - na cru-del',

d'a - spri tor - men - ti, e pe - ne sa - ran i tro-fei___ vostr', il

ro - go mi - o, i tro-fei vo - stri, il ro - - - - - - - - - - - - - - go mi - o.

| Interrotte speranze, e ferma fede, | Vain hopes and stout faith, flames and sharp darts in a frail heart; to nourish a fierce desire with sighs alone and hide your ill lest others see it; |
| Fiamme e strali possenti in debil core, |  |
| Nudrir sol di sospir un fer' ardore |  |
| E celar il tuo mal qual altri il vede; |  |

Interrotte speranze, e ferma fede,
Fiamme e strali possenti in debil core,
Nudrir sol di sospir un fer' ardore
E celar il tuo mal qual altri il vede;

Seguir di vago e fuggitivo piede
L'orme rivolte a voluntario errore,
Perder del seme spars' e'l frutto e'l fiore,
E la sperata gran languir mercede;

Far d'uno sguardo sol legge ai pensieri,
E d'un casto desio freno al desio,
E spender lagrimando i lustri intiere;

Questi, ch'à voi quasì gran fasci invio
Donna crudel, d'aspri tormenti e fieri
Saran i trofei vostri, il rogo mio.

G.-B. Guarini

Vain hopes and stout faith, flames and sharp darts in a frail heart; to nourish a fierce desire with sighs alone and hide your ill lest others see it;

To follow with frail and wavering foot the shadows which are willingly wrongful, to lose both fruit and flowers of the seed you have sown and the hoped-for pity for your languishing.

To make of a single glance the whole law of your thoughts and a rein to your desires from a chaste desire, and to spend whole days in weeping:

All these which I send to you like a large bouquet of torments and tortures, these, oh cruel lady, shall be your trophies as they are my torture!

12 · CLAUDIO MONTEVERDI (1567–1643),

*Interrotte speranze*

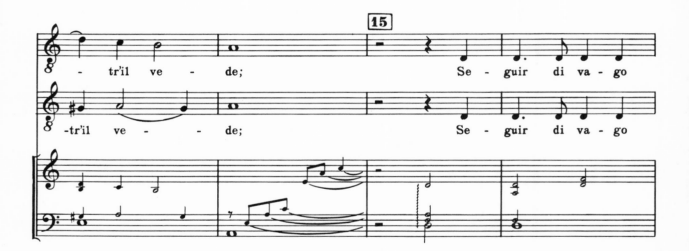

-ro - re, Per - der del se - me spar - so e'l frut - to e'l fio - re,

-ro - re, Per - der del se - me spar - so e'l frut - to e'l fio - re,

**25**

E la spe - ra - ta e gran lan-guir____ mer - ce - de; Far d'u-no sguar-do

E la spe - ra - ta e gran lan-guir mer - ce - de; Far d'u-no sguar-do

**30**

sol leg - ge ai pen - sie - ri, E d'un ca - sto vo - ler fre - no al de -

sol leg - ge ai pen - sie - ri, E d'un ca - sto vo - ler fre - no al de -

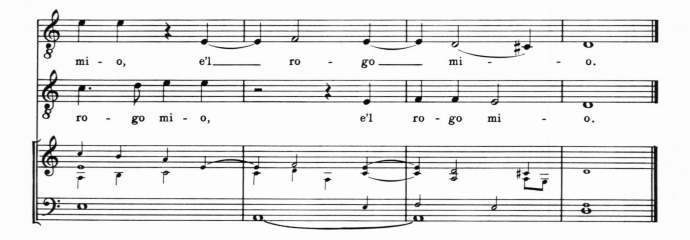

Interrotte speranze, eterna fede,
Fiamma e strali possenti in debil core,
Nutrir sol di sospir un fero ardore
E celar il suo mal quand' altr' il vede;
Seguir di vago e fuggitivo piede
L'orme rivolte à voluntario errore,
Perder del seme sparso e 'l frutto e 'l fiore,
E la sperata a gran languir mercede;
Far d'une sguardo sol legge ai pensieri,
E d'un casto voler freno al desio,
E spender lagrimando i lustri intiere;
Questi, ch'à voi quasì gran fasci invio
Donna crudel, d'aspri tormenti e fieri,
Saran i trofei vostri, e'l rogo mio.

*G.-B. Guarini*

Translation as in Number 11.

### 13 · SIGISMONDO D'INDIA  (ca. 1582–?),

*Mentre che'l cor*

[Molto moderato: recitando]

Men - tre che'l cor da gli a-mo - ro - si ver - mi  Fu con-su-

-ma - to e'n fiamm' a - mo-ros' ar - se,  Di va-ga fe - ra le ve-sti-gia spar-

5

-se Cer-cai per pog-gi so-li-ta-rio ed er - mi;  Ed eb-bi ar-dir, can-tan-do, di do-ler-mi d'A-

mi dis-ar-mo, Con stil ca-nu-to a-vrei fat - to, par-lan-do, Rom - per le pie-tre,

**20**

e pian-ger di dol-cez - za,— Rom-per le pie-tre,e pian-ger di dol-cez - za.

Mentre che'l cor degli amorosi vermi
Fu consumato e'n fiamm' amoros' arse,
Di vaga fera le vestiggia sparse
Cercai per poggi solitario ed hermi;
Ed ebbi ardir, cantando, di dolermi
D'Amor, di lei, che si dura m'apparse;
Ma l'ingegno e le rim' erano scarse
In quell' etade ai pensier nuovi e infermi.
Quel foco è mort' e 'l copr' un picciol marmo:
Che se col tempo fosse ito avanzando
Come già in altri, in fino alla vecchiezza;
Di rime armato ond' oggi mi disarmo,
Con stil canuto avrei fatto, parlando,
Romper le pietre, e pianger di dolcezza.

*F. Petrarch*

During the time my heart was gnawed by the worms of love, and burned in the flames of desire, I often followed the traces of a lovely creature over the solitary and deserted hills; and I was bold enough when I sang to complain of Love, of how harsh she seemed to me; but my wit and my rhyme were weak at that time to express the new strange thoughts. The fire is dead and covered with a small gravestone; if it had increased with time, as other things have, down to my old age, armed with verse which I have discarded now, in my mature style, it would, when it spoke, have made the very stones break and weep with pleasure.

## 14 · D'INDIA,

*O del cielo d'Amor*

**[Recitativo]**

O del Cie-lo d'A-mor u – ni-co so – le, Spec-chio de' se - mi-de - i,

**[a tempo]**

Al - tro rag-gio al tuo   lu - me al  tuo  dar - do, Ah ch'io  ar - do, ch'io   ar -

-do!   Deh, mi - ra-mi'n  vi - so, mia  gio - ia, mia   vi - ta, mio  ca - ro Te -

O del cielo d'Amor unico sole
Specchio de' semidei,
Altro raggi al tuo lume, al tuo dardo,
Ah, ch'io ardo, ch'io ardo!
Deh, mirami'n viso, mia gioia mia vita,
Mio caro Tesoro.
S'accese son io. Ahi, che mi struggo,
Mi sfaccio, mi moro, cor mio!

Oh, unique sun in the sky of love, mirror of the demi-gods! In your rays, your light, your darts, alas! I am burning, I am on fire! Woe is me! Look me in the face, my joy, my life, my dearest treasure; see how I am afire! Ah, how I struggle, how I strain; I am dying, my heart's love.

15 · STEFANO LANDI  (ca. 1590–1655),

*Superbi colli*

1ª parte [stilo recitativo]

Superbi colli, e voi, sa - cre ru - i - ne, Ch'il gran no - me di

Ro - ma an - cor te - ne - te, Ahi, che re - li - quie

mi - se - rand' a - ve - te di tan - te o - pe - re ec - cel - se   e

pel — le — gri — ne. Ahi, che re - li - quie mi - se -

-rand'_____ a - ve - te di tan - te o - pe - re ec - cel — se e

[più animato: espressivo]

pel — le — gri ne. Co - los — — —

— — — — - si, Ar - chi e Te - a - tri, O - pre __ di -

-vi - ne,　tri - on - fal pom-pe glo - ri - o - - - - - - - - - - - - - se e lie - te,

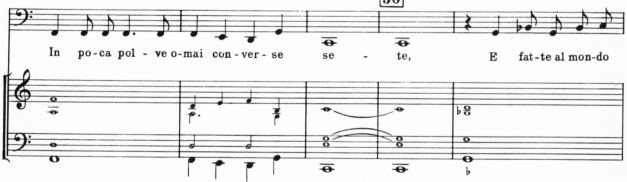

In po - ca pol - ve o-mai con - ver - se se - te,　E fat-te al mon-do

vil'　fa - - - - - - vo -la al fi - ne.

In po - ca pol - - - - ve o - mai con - ver - se____

se - te, e fa - - - - - t'al mon - do vil'

fa - - - - - - - - vo la al fi - - ne.

Superbi colli, e voi sacre ruine
Ch'il gran nome di Roma ancor tenete,
Ahi, che reliquie miserand' avete
di tante opere eccelse e pellegrine.
Colossi, Archi e Teatri,
Opere divine, trionfal pompe gloriose e liete,
In poca polve homai converse sete,
E fatte al monde vil' favola al fine.

Proud hills, and you, sacred ruins
Which still bear the great name of Rome,
Ah, what miserable relics remain
of mighty works and pilgrims.
Colossal arches and theatres, divine works,
Triumphal pomp, glorious and joyful,
Now are turned to a little dust, and at the last
have become for the world a tawdry story.

## 16 · CLAUDIO SARACENI (1586–ca. 1649),

*Da te parto*

[Very freely; molto moderato]

Da te par - to cor mi - o, Da te par - to cor mi - o:

io va - do, a - ni-ma mi - a, io va - do, a - ni-ma mi - a,

Pe - re-grin sco-no-sciu - to, D'i-gno-ti li - di ha-bi-tar l'a - re - ne.

Er - me, cam-pa-gne, ab-ban-do-na - ti or-ro - ri Sa - ran del-le mie pe - ne,

Da te parto, cor mio, io vado, anima mia
Peregrin sconosciuto,
D'ignoti lidi habitar l'arene.
Erme, campagne abbandonati, horrori
Saran delle mie pene
De' miei passati ardori
Dell'idol mio perduto.
Ecco misero e flebile e dolente
Del mio duol, del mio ardir,
Memoria ardente.

I leave thee, my heart, I go from thee, my soul, an unknown wanderer to inhabit strange sandy shores. Rocks, abandoned fields, horrors, will be my penance for past ardor for my lost idol. Here, miserable, lamenting, and sorrowful from my grief, my ardor, the flame of memory, burns.

## 17 · SARACENI,

*Mori, mi dice*

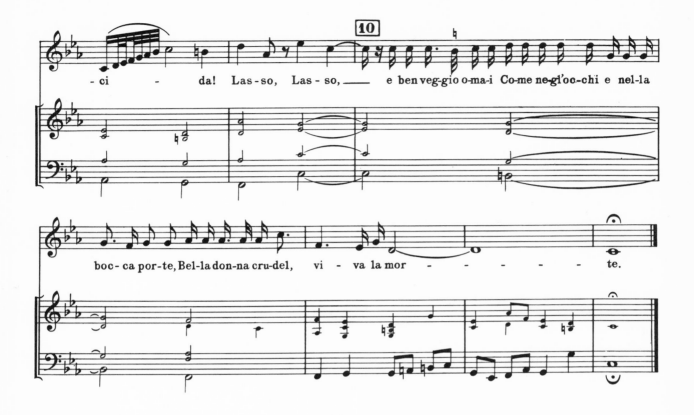

-ci - da! Las-so, Las - so, ___ e ben veg-gio o-ma-i Co-me ne-gl'oc-chi e nel-la

boc- ca por-te, Bel-la don-na cru-del, vi - va la mor - - - - - te.

Mori, mi dice, e mentre
Con quel guardo crudel morir mi fai,
Con quel dolce parlar vita mi dai.
Ah, che vita omicida,
Che mi tien vivo sol perche m'ancida!
Lasso, lasso, e ben veggio omai
Come negl'occhi e nella bocca porte,
Bella donna crudel, viva la morte.

"Die," you say to me, and as you slay me with that cruel glance you give me life with sweet speech. Alas, what a murderous life it is that keeps me alive only to kill me! Woe is me! Now I perceive that a fair, cruel lady in her eyes and in her mouth bears living death.

## 18 · ALESSANDRO GRANDI  (?–1630),

*O quam tu pulchra es*

O - cu - li tu - i co-lum-ba - rum, ca-pel-li tu - i si - cut gre - ges ca-pra-

-rum et den-ti tu - i si-cut gre - ges ton-sa - rum. O_____ quam tu pul-chra

es. Ve - ni, ve - ni de Li - ba - no, ve - ni, ve - ni de

Li - ba - no, ve - ni a - mi - ca me - a, co - lum - ba me - a, for-

[meno mosso: espressivo]

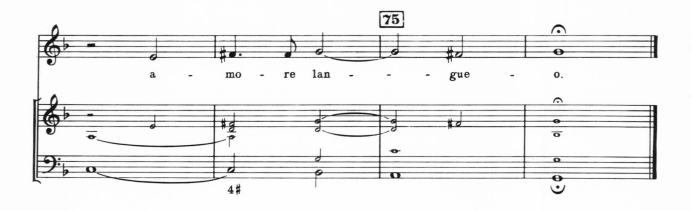

a - mo - re lan - - gue - o.

(The text is based on the *Song of Songs* and is a free rendition of vv.1-2,8.)

O quam tu pulchra es, O quam pulchra es, quam pulchra es amica mea, quam pulchra es columba mea, quam pulchra es formosa mea, O quam tu pulchra es! Oculi tui columbarum, capelli tui sicut greges caprarum et denti tui sicut greges tonsarum. O quam tu pulchra es, Veni, veni de Libano, veni amica mea, columba mea, formosa mea. O quam tu pulchra es, veni, veni coronaberis. Surge, surge propera, surge, sponsa mea, surge dilecta mea, surge immaculata mea. Surge, veni, veni, veni, Quia amore langueo.

How beautiful thou art, my love! How beautiful thou art, my dove, my pretty one! Your eyes are like a dove's, your hair is like a flock of goats, your teeth like a flock of ewes ready for shearing. Come from Lebanon, my love, my dove, my pretty one! How beautiful thou art, come—Arise, arise my bride, arise my delight, arise my spotless one. Arise and come, for I am sick with love.

## 19 · GIACOMO CARISSIMI (1605–1674),

*Nò, nò, mio core*

ma - re,          non fi - dar - ti,       non fi - dar - ti  a  que - sta  cal -

- - ma  Ch'ha ri - dot - - ta  più _____ d'un al - ma  di - spe - ra -

- - - - - - - - ta  à  nau - fra - ga - - re.  Ch'ha ri -

- dot - - ta  più _____ d'un  al - ma  di - spe - ra - -

ta à nau-fra-ga - re. Non la -

35
-sciar - ti ___ lu - sin - ga - re ___ da si dol - ce ___

40
pro - spet - ti - va, ___ che lon - ta - no ___ del la

45
ri - va ___ por - ti ri - schio d'an -

**50**

-ne - gar - ti. Che lon - ta - no___ del - la ri - va___

**55**

por - ti ri - - - - - - schio d'an - ne - gar -

**60** [Tempo Iº]

-ti. Nò, nò, mio co - re nò, nò, non___ in - gol -

**65**

-far - ti, non___ in - gol - far - ti, No -

- - i l'a-mi-co li - do, e con ven - - to il più so-

-a - ve. La-sce-ra - - - - - - i L'a-mi-co Li - do

Nò, nò, mio core, nò,
non ingolfarti.
Se d'amor t'è noto il mare,
non fidarti
a questa calma
ch'ha ridotta più d'un alma
disperata à naufragare.
Non lasciarti lusingare
da si dolce prospettiva,
che lontano della riva
porti rischio d'annegarti.
Nò, nò, mio core . . .
Non ti fidi à stelle, à luna
il nocchier del tuo pensiero,
che in quel pelago si fiero
sempre corresi fortuna.
Partirai con volo ardito
del desio su la tua nave,
e con vento il più soave
lascerai l'amico lido.

No, no! my heart, no!
Do not be engulfed!
If the sea of love is strange to you,
do not trust yourself
to that calm
which has brought many a despairing soul
to shipwreck.
Do not be deceived
by such a pleasant sight,
because far from the shore
you run the risk of drowning.
No, no! my heart!
Do not trust the stars, the moon,
the pilot of your thoughts,
for in this treacherous sea
a tempest is always near.
You will set sail upon your ship
with the strong sails of your desire
and with the gentlest winds
you will leave the friendly shore.

## 20 · PIETRO FRANCESCO CAVALLI (1602–1676),

*Tremulo spirito* (Hecuba's lament)

Tremulo spirito, flebile e languido,
escivi subito.

Volati, l'anima ch'Erebo
torbido, cupido, aspetta là.

Povero Priamo, scordati d'Hecuba,
vedova misera.

Causano l'ultimo horrido esilio,
Paride ed Elena.

Tremulous spirit, weeping and weary,
go quickly;

Fly, spirit, that turbid and greedy Erebus awaits.

Poor Priamus, forget Hecuba, forlorn widow:

Paris and Helen cause the final terrible exile.

## 21 · PIETRO ANTONIO CESTI (1623–1669),

*Bella Clori*

Bel - la Clo - ri, an - cor non cre - di Ciò che ve - di.

Se non cu - ri il par - lar mi - o, Ve - di il pra - to e

sen - ti il __ ri - - o, Ed a - scol - ta __ le pa -

-ro - le Che ti di - ce il ma - - - - -

[Recitativo]

Ma, se'l pra-to, se'l ri-o, Se'l ma - re e'l so - le Non ha vo - ce ba-stan - te

[Ms. m. 147]

[6]

A dir -ti il ve - ro, At - ten - di il mio pen-sie - - ro.

[Aria]

Si_ri_schia-ra il ri - o tur-ba-to__ E più va - go il sol_____

__ri - sor - ge; Vien tran-quil-lo il ma - re_i - ra - to, Ed il pra-to,

[7    6]

ed il pra-to, nu-do un tem-po di fior, nu-do un tem-po di fior.     Di

fior__ s'a-dor __ na;     Ma _____ la bel-lez __ za tua

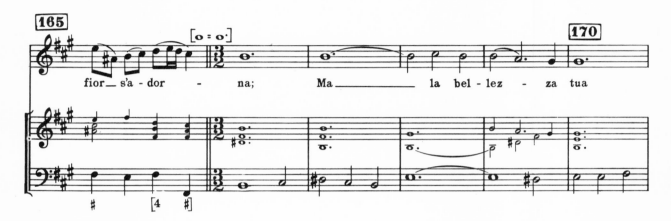

par __ __ te, Non tor-na,     par __ __ te, Non

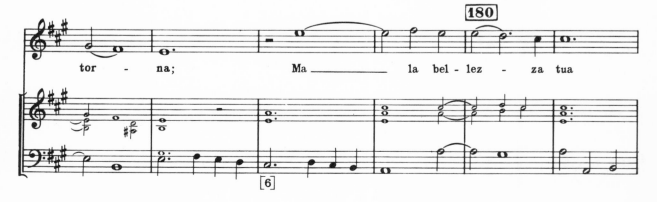

tor __ na;     Ma _____ la bel-lez __ za tua

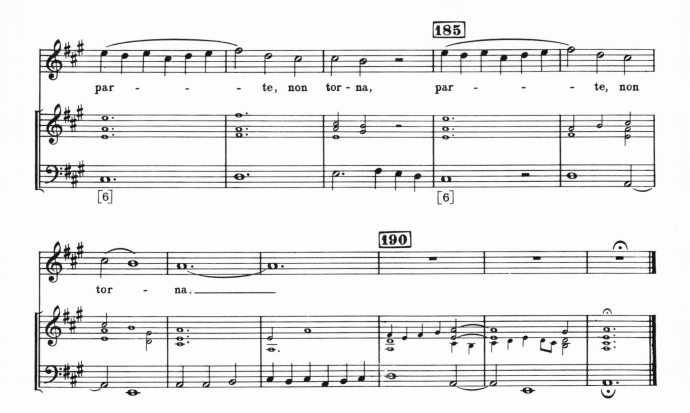

Bella Clori, ancor non credi
Ciò che vedi.
Se non curi il parlar mio,
Vedi il prato e senti il rio,
Ed ascolta le parole
Che ti dice il mare e'l sole.
D'amaranto ricco manto
Se m'inganna April' ridente,
Poco dura mia ventura
Al soffiar di bocca algente.
E tu Clori nol comprendi
Ciò ch'intendi.

Ma se'l prato, se'l rio,
Se'l mare e'l sole
Non ha voce bastante
A dirti il vero,
Attendi il mio pensiero.
Si rischiara il rio turbato
E più vago il sol risorge;
Vien tranquillo il mar irato,
Ed il prato, nudo un tempo,
Di fior s'adorna;
Ma la bellezza tua parte,
Non torna.

Fair Chloris, you still do not believe what you see.
If you do not believe what I say, look at the
meadow, and listen to the brook, and hearken to
the words that the sea and the and the sun utter.
If smiling April deceives me with her green man-
tle, my good fortune lasts but a short while when
the cold winds blow. And you, Chloris, do not understand what you hear!

But if the voices of the meadow, the brook, the
sea and the sun are not sufficient to tell you the
truth, listen to my thoughts!

The turbid brook will become clear again, the
sun will rise brighter, the raging sea will grow
calm, and the meadow, once bare, will be adorned
with flowers; but your beauty departs, never to
return.

## 22 · LUIGI ROSSI (ca. 1598–1653),

*La Gelosia*

[Molto espressivo: non troppo lento]

1. Ge - lo-si - a,    che a po-co a    po-co nel mio cor_____ ser -
2. Ma    cru-del,    tu pur pian    pia-no del mio cor_____

-pen - - - - do_____                        va -
_____ stai    sul - le    por - - -

- i,    Non en-trar    dov' ar - de il fo - co,    Ve-ro a-mor, ve-ro a-mor non_ ge - la_
- te,    Fug-gi, fug - gi, oi - mè,    lon - ta - no,    Del tuo gel', del tuo ge-lo è A-mor_ più_

* The notes with stems down are for the 2nd verse.

ma - i,      Non en - trar dov' ar - de il    fo-co, Ve-ro a-mor,  ve-ro a-mor__ non__ ge - la__
for - te,      Fug-gi, fug-gi, oi - mè,  lon - ta-no, Del tuo gel', del tuo  ge - lo è A-mor__ più__

ma - i, mai,__ mai,__  mai,__  Ve-ro a-mor,  ve-ro a-mor non__  ge - la ma - i,
for-te, Fug - gi, fug__ gi lon-ta - no,  fug - gi lon-ta - no, Del tuo  ge - lo e A-mor__ più__

ma - i,      Non_____ ge - la ma - i.
for - te   è A-mor_____ più for - te.

Da me che

Lascia-mi ge-lo-si - a! Lascia-mi

ge - lo - si - a! La - scia-mi,   la-scia-mi ge - lo - si - a!

ge - - - - - - - - - - - - - - - -

- lo - - - - - - si - a!

1.

Gelosia, che a poco a poco
Nel mio cor serpendo vai,
Non entrar dov' arde il foco,
Vero amor non gela mai.
Da me che brami?
Forse vuoi tu
Ch'io più non ami.
Furia dell'alma mia!
Non mi tormentar più!
Lasciami gelosia!

Jealousy, which creeps serpent-like into my heart, do not enter where burns the fire of true love; true love never chills, never, never.

What do you want of me? Perhaps you wish me to cease loving! Fury of my soul! Cease to torment me! No more! No more! Depart from me, Jealousy, depart!

2.

Ma crudel, tu pur pian piano
Del mio cor stai sulle porte.
Fuggi, fuggi, oimè, lontano
Del tuo gel è Amor più forte.
Da me che brami?
Godendo io sto
De' miei pensieri.
Furia dell'alma mia!
Non più rigor, no, no!
Lasciami gelosia.

But cruel, you remain quietly at the gates of my heart. Flee, flee from me. Love is stronger than your icy chill. What do you want of me? I am happy with my thoughts. My soul's fury, constrain me not. No, no, no! Leave me, Jealousy, depart, depart!

## 23 · BARBARA STROZZI (1620–?),

*Lagrime mie*

La - - - - - - - - gri-me mi - e,

à che vi____ trat-te - ne - - - - te, Per-

-che non i-sfo-ga-te il fier, il fier do - lo - - - - -

che per mia ca - gio-ne, per mia ca - gio-ne pro-va ma - le    il _____ mi - o be -

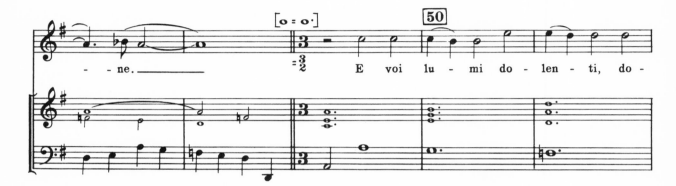

- - ne. _____    E  voi  lu - mi  do - len - ti,  do-

-len -  ti, e  voi  lu - mi  do - len - ti,  do - len -  ti,    non  pian -

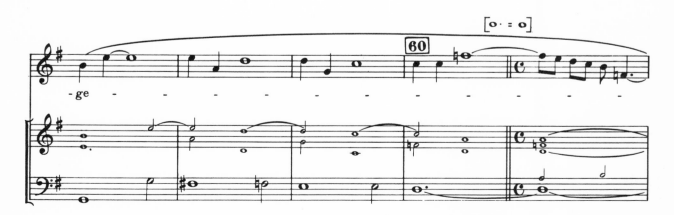

-ge - - - - - - - - - - -

**[Tempo I°]**

te! La - - - - - - - gri-me mi - e, à che, à che vi trat-te-ne - te?

**Aria**

1. Li-dia, ahi-mè, veg-go man-car-mi, Li-dia, ahi-mè, veg-go man-car - mi. L'i-dol
2. Se la mor - te m'è gra - di -ta, se la mor - te m'è gra - di - ta, Or che

mio, che tan to a do - - - - - ro, Stà co - lei tra du - ri mar-mi per cui
son pri -va di spe - - - - - ne, Dhè to - glie-te -mi la vi- ta (Ve ne

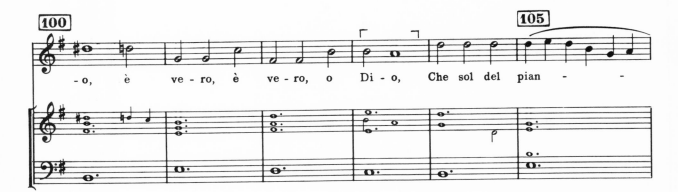

Lagrime mie, à che vi trattenete,
Perchè non isfogate il fier' dolore,
Chi mi toglie 'l respiro e opprime il core?

Lidia, che tant' adoro,
Perchè un guardo pietoso, ahimè, mi donò,
Il paterno rigor l'impriggionò.
Tra due mura rinchiusa stà la bella innocente,
Dove giunger non può raggio di sole,
E quel che più mi duole
Ed accresc'il mio mal, tormenti e pene,
È che per mia cagione prova male il mio bene.
E voi lume dolenti non piangete!
Lagrime mie, à che vi trattenete?

Lidia, ahimè, veggo mancarmi. L'idol mio,
Che tanto adoro,
Stà colei tra duri marmi per cui spiro
E pur non moro.
Se la morte m'è gradita,
Or che son privo di spene,
Dhè, toglietemi la vita
(Ve ne prego) aspre mie pene.
Ma ben m'accorgo, che per tormentarmi
maggiormente, La sorte mi niega anco la morte.
Se dunque è vero, o Dio, che sol del pianto mio,
Il rio destino ha sete.

Tears of mine, why do you hold back, why don't you wash away the pain which deprives me of breath and oppresses my heart?

Lidia whom I adore, because she gave me a pitying glance, has been imprisoned by her father's severity. The innocent girl is locked up within walls which the sun's rays cannot penetrate, and what pains me most, and increases my torment, is that it is because of me that my beloved is suffering. And you, eyes of mine, are not weeping! What are you waiting for?

Alas, how I miss my Lidia, my idol I love so much! She is shut up within marble walls and I sigh but do not die! If death might be granted to me now that I have no hope, take my life, I beg of you, oh my sufferings! But I am well aware that in order to torture me even more, Fate even denies me death. It is true then, oh God, that destiny desires only my tears.

## 24 · ALESSANDRO STRADELLA (1642–1682),

*S'Amor m'annoda il piede*

ser - vi-tù,        più non cu - ro il mio do - lo-re, vi-vo lie - to in

ser - vi-tù, in ser - vi - tù, vi-vo lie - to in ser - vi - tù.        Il mio

cor già ___ fat - to au - da - ce ___ Sprez - za ogn' or' l'ar - den - te

fa - - - ce,        Sprez - - za ogn'        or'  l'ar - den - te

fa - - - - - - - - - ce  Che per un

va - go og - get - to,  che per un  va - go og - get - to,  Ogn' in -

-cen-dio d'a - mo - - re è  gio-ia à un pet - to.  Ogn' in -

-cen-dio d'a - mo - - re è  gio - ia,  è  gio-ia à un pet -

S'Amor m'annoda il piede
Come dunque fuggirò
Da quel cor che non ha fede?
Libertà non spero, no.
Sian pur dure le catene,
Dure in sempre le mie pene,
Ch'in servitù costante
God' ogn' ora languendo un core amante.
Lo stral ch'io porto al core
D'un bel guardo colpo fù.
Più non curo il mio dolore,
Vivo lieto in servitù.
Il mio cor già fatto audace
Sprezza ogn' or' l'ardente face;
Che per vago oggetto
Ogn' incendio d'amore è gioia à un petto.

If Love chains my feet, how can I flee from that faithless heart? I cannot hope for liberty. No matter how harsh the shackles, my suffering continues always, for in eternal servitude a loving heart enjoys its languishing.

The arrow I bear in my heart was the fault of a beautiful glance; I no longer regret my servitude, but live happily in slavery. My loving heart, now brave, disdains the burning torch, because every fire of love for a sweet object is joy to the heart.

## 25 · ALESSANDRO SCARLATTI (1660–1725),

*Goderai sempre, crudele*

Dim-mi al - me-no in che pec-cai, che se

po - i mor - te, mor - te mi da - i, mi

da - i, stra - li, dar - di in-con-tre - rò, in - con - tre-rò, ____

____ in - con - tre-rò. Go - de-ra - i sem-pre cru-

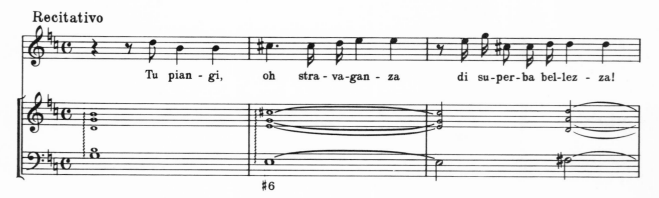

Chi t'a - mi fug-gi, e se-gui chi ti sprez - za. Bel - la, se bra-mi

pa - ce, scac-cia da no-bil co - re quell' i - ma-go cru-de - le che, sor-da a miei que -

-re - le, col stral col - mo di fiel, col stral col - mo di fiel, v'im-pres - se A -

-mo - re.

**45** Aria. Allegro

Se vuoi pa-ce o di-let - to          Se vuoi pa-ce o di-let -to   tor -

-na,   tor - na col pri-mo af - fet-to,   mia bel-la,a so - spi-rar,____

mia bel - la,a_ so - spi - rar,   mia bel - la,a_ so - spi - rar.

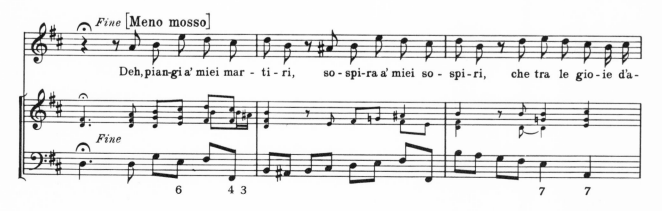

Deh, pian-gi a' miei mar - ti - ri,   so - spi-ra a' miei so - spi - ri,   che tra le gio - ie d'a-

-mor, che tra le gio - ie d'a - mor dol - ce, dol - ce, dol - ce è il pe-

*Da capo al Fine*

- nar,_____ dol-ce è il pe-nar,__dol - ce è il pe-nar, dol - ce, dol - ce è il pe-nar.

[Recitativo]

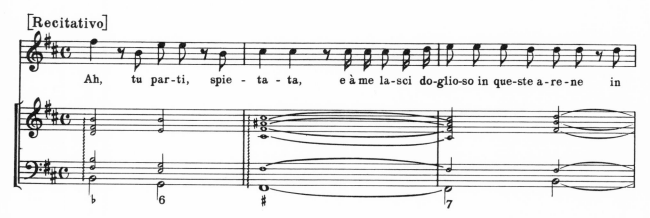

Ah, tu par-ti, spie - ta-ta, e à me la-sci do-glio-so in que-ste a-re-ne in

[Aria. Andante con moto]

brac-cio al - le mie pe-ne. Al-men,co' tuoi bei ra - i

Mi - ra, mi - ra___ la mor - te mi - a,

♭ 6   #6   6   #6

#6

**75**

e poi t'en va - - - - i, e poi t'en va -

6  6  #6  6  #6      6  6  #6      5  6      #6

**80**

-i,  e poi,  e poi t'en va - - - i.      Mi - ra, mi - ra___

6      6  #6      #6      #6  6

**85**

la mor - te mi - a,      e poi t'en va - - - i, e

#6  6  #6  4  3      6      #6  6  #6

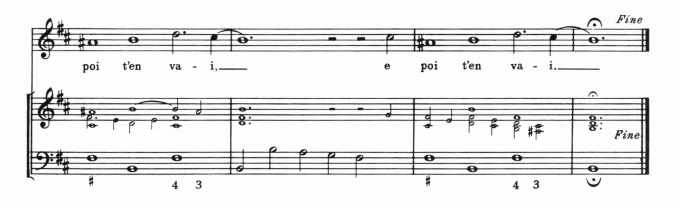

### Aria I

Goderai sempre, crudele,
a' miei pianti, alle querele
d'un amante, che costante, t'adorò.
Dimmi almeno in che peccai,
che se poi morte me dai,
strali, dardi incontrerò.
    Goderai . . . etc.

You will always take pleasure, cruel that you are,
in my weeping, in the struggles of a constant lover
who adores you. At least tell me in what I erred,
for if later you slay me, I shall encounter darts
and arrows.

### Recitativo

Tu piangi, oh stravaganza di superba
bellezza; chi t'ama fuggi, e segui chi
ti prezza. Bella, se brami pace, scaccia
da nobil core quell' imago crudele che,
sorda a' miei querele, col stral colmo
di fiel v'impresse Amore.

You are weeping, oh strange action for proud
beauty; you flee him who loves you and follow
him who hates you. Oh beautiful one, if you desire peace, drive from your noble heart this cruel
image which, deaf to my protests, Love inflicted
upon you with his arrows tipped with poison.

### Aria II

Se vuoi pace o diletto,
torna col primo affetto,
mia bella, a sospirar.
Dhe, piangi a' miei martiri,
sospira a' miei sospiri,
che tra le gioie d'amor
dolce, dolce è 'l penar.

If you desire peace or happiness, my lovely, return
to sighing with your first love. Alas, weep at my
suffering, sigh with my sighs; for sweet it is to suffer amid the joys of love.

### Recitativo and Aria III

Ah, tu parti, spietata
e à me lasci doglioso in queste arene
in braccio alle mie pene.
Almen co' tuoi bei rai,
Mira la morte mia e poi t'en vai.

Ah! you are departing, pitiless girl, and you leave
me sorrowing in this desert in the embrace of my
pain. At least, with your lovely eyes, look upon
my death and then depart.

## 26 · BENEDETTO MARCELLO (1686–1739),

*Dal tribunal augusto*

Dal Tri - bu-nal au - gu-sto, o - ve tu sie - di, O_____ di giu-sti - zia_____

Fon - te, O Fon-te di cle - men - za, l'al - to giu-di - zio a-spet - -

- to, l'al - to giu - di - zio a-spet - to, dal Tri - bu-nal au -

-gu-sto, o - ve tu sie - di, O_____ di giu-sti - zia Fon-te, O    Fon-te

di cle - men - za,    l'al - to giu-di - zio a-spet ____ - to,  l'al-to giu-

-di - zio, l'al - to giu-di - zio a-spet - to.                        Di

là    la mia ra - gion    d'u-dir-ti de - gna,  e  si de-ci-da al-fin,   e

si de-ci-da al-fin la cau - sa mi - a, e si de-ci-da al-fin, e si de-ci-da al-

-fin la cau - sa___ mi - a.

**Largo**

Da un po-po-lo che à te non fu, non___ fu mai sa - cro, per pie-tà, per pie-

-tà mi di-fen - di, e dagl'in-gan-ni i-ni-qui e dal-le fro-di di quel che lo go-ver-na in-giu-sto,

Dal Tribunal augusto ove tu siedi, O di giustizia Fonte, O Fonte di clemenza, l'alto giudizio aspetto. Di là la mia ragion d'udirti degna, e si decida alfin la causa mia. Da un popolo che à te non fu mai sacro, per pietà mi difendi; e dagl' inganni iniqui e dalle frodi di quel che lo governa ingiusto, Rege, fa che disciolto tua mercede, io resti.

From the high tribunal where thou art seated, O fount of justice, O fount of mercy, I await thy supreme judgment. From there deign to hear my complaint and at last decide my case. In pity defend me from a people never sacred to thee; and by thy mercy, O King, free me from the evil tricks and deceits of him who reigns against all justice.

*Ps. 42:1*

PART II

# Songs by English Composers

## 27 · ANONYMOUS,

*Willow Song*

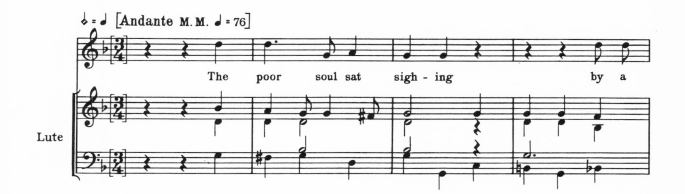

The poor soul sat sigh - ing by a

sick - a - more tree, Sing wil - lo, wil - lo, wil - lo!

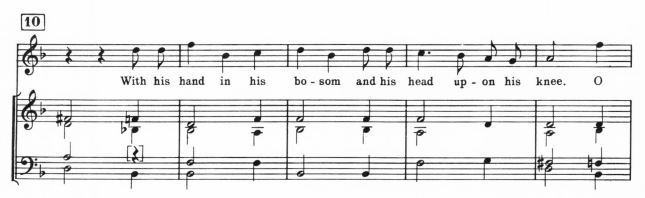

With his hand in his bo - som and his head up - on his knee. O

The poor soul sat sighing by a sickamore tree,
Sing willo, willo, willo!
With his hand in his bosom and his head upon
    his knee.
O willo, willo, willo, willo, shall be my garland.
Sing all a green willo, willo, willo, willo,
Aye me, sing green willo must be my garland.

He sighed in his singing and made a great moan,
    Sing . . .
I am dead to all pleasure, my true love she is
    gone. O willo . . .
The mute bird sat by him, was made tame by his
    moans;
The true tears fell from him would have melted

the stones.

Come all you forsaken and mourn ye with me;
Who speaks of a false love, mine's falser than she.

Let love no more boast her in palace nor bower,
It buds, but it blasteth ere it be a flower.

Thou fair and most false, I die with thy wound;
Thou hast lost the truest lover that goeth on the
    ground.

Let nobody chide her, her scorn I approve;
She was born to be false, and I to die for love.

Take this for my farewell and latest adieu.
Write this on my tomb, that in love I was true.

## 28 · THOMAS MORLEY (ca. 1557–1603),

*Come, Sorrow, come*

1. Come,___ Sor - row, come, sit down and mourn with me; Hang down thy head up-on thy bale - ful breast That God and man and all the world___ ___ may see Our hea - vy hearts do live in qui - et rest.

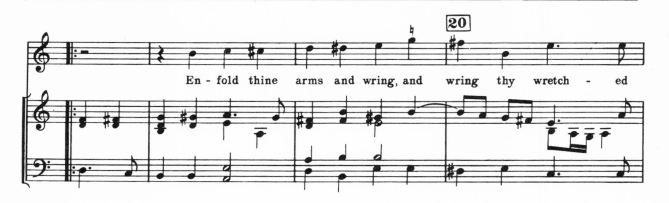

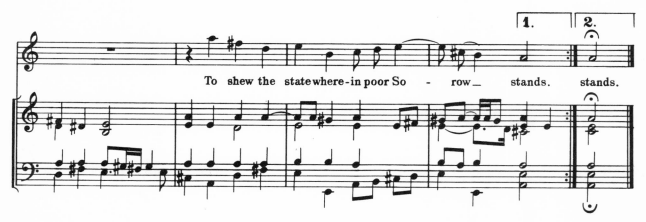

1. Come, Sorrow, come, sit down and mourn with me;
   Hang down thy head upon thy baleful breast
   That God and man and all the world may see
   Our heavy hearts do live in quiet rest.
   Enfold thine arms and wring thy wretched hands,
   To shew the state wherein poor Sorrow stands.
2. Cry not out-right, for that were children's guise,
   But let thy tears fall trickling down thy face;

And weep so long until thy blubbered eyes
May see (in sum) the depth of thy disgrace.
O shake thy head, but not a word but mum;
The heart once dead, the tongue is stroken dumb.
3. And let our fare be dishes of despite
   To break our hearts and not our fasts withal;
   Then let us sup with sorrow sops at night
   And bitter sauce, all of a broken gall.
   Thus let us live till heavens may rue to see
   The doleful doom ordained for thee and me.

## 29 · PHILIP ROSSETER (c. 1575–1623),

*And would you see my mistress' face*

And would you see my mistress' face?
It is a flow'ry garden place
Where knots of beauties have such grace
That all is work and nowhere space.

It is a sweet delicious morn
Where day is breeding, never born.
It is a meadow yet unshorn
Whom thousand flowers do adorn.

It is the heavens' bright reflex,
Weak eyes to dazzle and to vex;

It is the Idaea of her sex,
Envy of whom doth world perplex.

It is a face of death that smiles,
Pleasing, though it kills the whiles,
Where death and love in pretty wiles
Each other naturally beguiles.

It is fair beauty's freshest youth,
It is the feigned Elysium's truth,
The Spring that wintered hearts reneweth;
And this is that my soul pursueth.

## 30 · JOHN DOWLAND (1563–1620),

*If that a sinner's sighs*

If that a sinner's sighs be Angels' food,
Or that repentant tears be Angels' wine,
Accept, O Lord, in this most pensive mood

These hearty sighs and doleful plaints of mine
That went, like Peter, forth most sinfully,
But not, as Peter did, weep, weep bitterly.

### 31 · DOWLAND,

*Lady, if you so spite me*

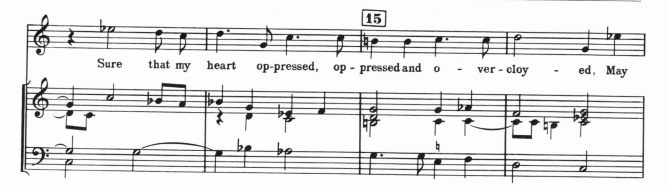

Sure that my heart op-pressed, op-pressed and o - ver-cloy - ed, May

break, May ___ break thus o - ver-joyed, o - ver - joy - ed?

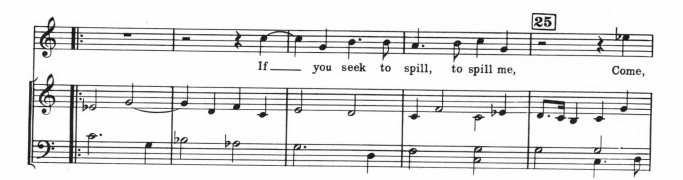

If ___ you seek to spill, to spill me, Come,

kiss me sweet, come kiss me sweet, come kiss me sweet, and kill me.

So shall your heart, your heart your heart be eas - ed,

And I shall rest con-tent and ___ die,    and ___

die _____ well pleas - - - ed.

Lady, if you so spite me,
Wherefore do you so oft kiss and delight me,
Sure that my heart oppressed and overcloyed
May break, thus overjoyed?
If you seek to spill me
Come, kiss me, sweet, and kill me.
So shall your heart be eased,
And I shall rest content and die well pleased.

## 32 · WILLIAM CORKINE (fl. in the early 17th century),

*Each lovely grace*

Each lovely grace my Lady doth possess,
Let all men view, and in their view admire
In whose sweet breast all virtuous thoughts do
    rest;
Zealous to pity, chaste in her own desire,
And do make up a rare and worthy creature
Both wise and chaste and fair in form and feature.
Enter but into thought of her, perfection thou
    wilt confess,
Thou wilt confess, and in confessing prove
How none deserves like praise, nor yet like love.

## 33 · CORKINE,

*Beauty sat bathing*

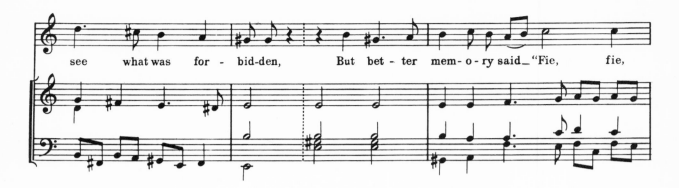

see    what was    for - bid-den,    But  bet - ter  mem- o - ry said  "Fie,    fie,

fie,    fie,    fie,    fie, fie,  fie, fie,  fie, fie,  fie, fie,

fie, So vaine de - sire was chid-den, So  vaine  de - sire was  chid - den.

Beauty sat bathing by a spring
Where fairest shades did hide her.
The winds blew calme, the birds did sing,
The cool streams ran beside her.
My wanton thoughts enticed my eye
To see what was forbidden,
But better memory said "Fie, fie,"
So vaine desire was chidden.

Into a slumber then I fell,
But fond imagination
Seem'd to see, but could not tell,
Her feature or her fashion.
But even as babes in dreams do smile,
And sometimes fall aweeping:
So I awoke as wise the while
As when I fell a-sleeping.

*Anthony Munday*

## 34 · ROBERT JOHNSON (?–1633),

*Care-charming sleep*

loud, Or    pain - full    to _____ his slum-bers, but eas - y,

sweet, And as    a    purl - ing ___ stream, you    son    of    Night,

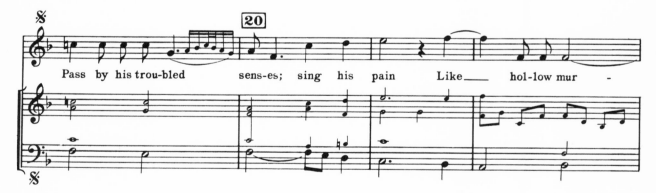

Pass  by  his trou-bled    sens-es; sing his  pain    Like ___ hol-low mur -

- mur-ing winds,  or  sil - - - ver rain;   In - to ____ this ___

Prince gent-ly, o gent-ly, o gent-ly slide And

kiss him in - to slum-ber like ————— a ————— bride.

Care-charming sleep, thou easer of all woes,
Brother of Death, sweetly thyself dispose
On this afflicted wight; fall like a cloud
In gentle showers; give nothing that is loud
Or painful to his slumbers, but easy, sweet,
And as a purling stream, you son of Night,
Pass by his troubled senses; sing his pain
Like hollow-murmuring winds, or silver rain;
Into this Prince gently, o gently slide
And kiss him into slumber like a bride.

## 35 · GEORGE JEFFRIES (?–1685),

*Praise the Lord, O my soul*

Praise___ the Lord, O my soul, Praise___

___ the Lord, O my soul, O Lord my

God, Thou art be-come ___ ex-ceed-ing glo - ri - ous, O Lord my God, Thou

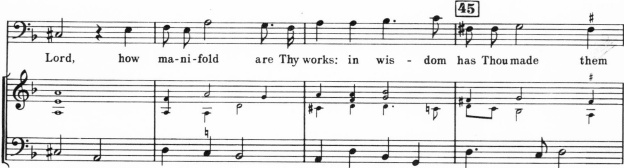

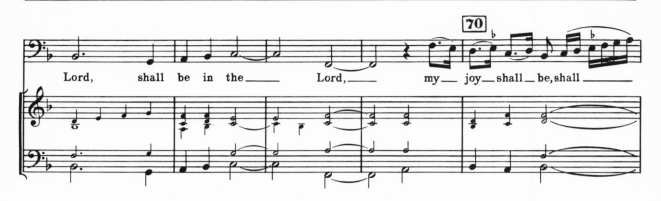

Lord,    shall be in the___    Lord,___    my___ joy___ shall_ be, shall___

be in the Lord.    Al - le - lu - - - - - -

- ia, Al - le - lu - ia.    Al - le - lu -

- - - - - ia,    Al - le - lu - -

Praise the Lord, O my soul, O Lord my God, thou art become exceeding glorious. Thou art clothed with majesty and honor. Thou deckest Thyself with light as it were with a garment, And spreadest out the Heavens like a curtain. O Lord, how manifold are thy works: in wisdom has Thou made them all. The Earth is full of Thy riches. I will sing unto the Lord as long as I live, I will praise my God whilst I have my being; And so shall my words please Him, my joy shall be in the Lord. Alleluia.

*Ps. 104*

## 36 · HENRY LAWES (1596–1662),

*The Lark*

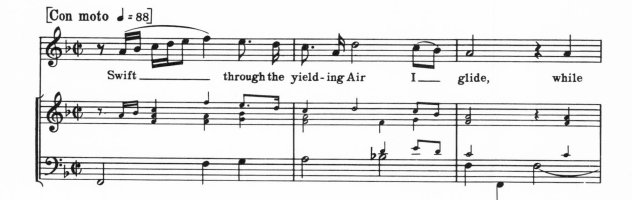

Swift _____ through the yield-ing Air I _____ glide,    while

nights    shall be, shades  a-bide;    Yet in my flight _____ (tho'ne'er so fast)    I

Tune    and Time _____    the wild _____ winds'_ blast:    And ere the Sun be come a-

Swift through the yielding Air I glide,
while nights shall be, shades abide;
Yet in my flight (though ne'er so fast)
I Tune and Time the wilde winds blast:
And ere the Sun be come about,
Teach the young Lark his Lesson out;
who early as the Day is born
sings his shrill Anthem to the rising morn;
Let never mortal lose the pains
to imitate my Aiery strains,
whose pitch, too high for human ears
was set me by the tuneful Spheres.
I carol to the Fairies' King,
Wake him a-mornings when I sing:
And when the Sun stoops to the deep,
Rock him again and his fair Queen asleep.

*Dryden and Lee*

37 · H. LAWES,

*Go, lovely Rose*

[Andante espressivo]

1. Go, love-ly Rose, tell her that wastes _____ her time and me,
2. Small is the worth of beau-ty from _____ the light re-tir'd,

that now she knows, when I re-sem-ble her to thee, how sweet and fair she
Bid her come forth, Suf-fer her-self to be de-sir'd, and not _____ blush to

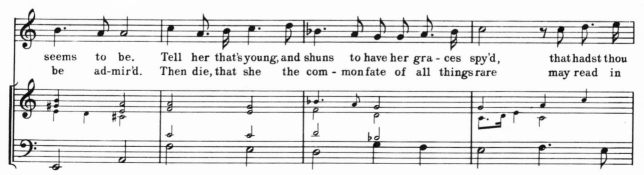

seems to be. Tell her that's young, and shuns to have her gra-ces spy'd, that hadst thou
be ad-mir'd. Then die, that she the com-mon fate of all things rare may read in

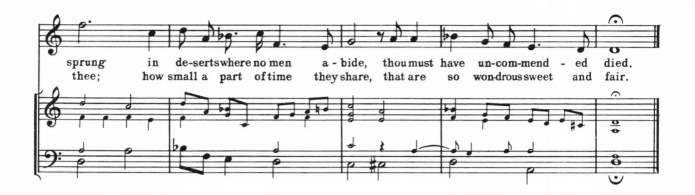

sprung         in  de-serts where no men     a - bide,  thou must have  un-com-mend  -  ed   died.
thee;          how small a  part of time     they share,  that are     so  won-drous sweet   and   fair.

Go, lovely Rose,
tell her that wastes her time and me,
that now she knows,
when I resemble her to thee,
how sweet and fair she seems to be.
Tell her that's young,
and shuns to have her graces spy'd,
that hadst thou sprung
in deserts where no men abide,
thou must have uncommended died.

Small is the worth
of beauty from the light retir'd,
Bid her come forth,
Suffer herself to be desir'd,
and not blush to be admir'd.
Then die, that she
the common fate of all things rare
may read in thee;
how small a part of time they share,
that are so wondrous sweet and fair.

*Edmund Waller*

38 · WILLIAM LAWES (1602–1645),

*Had you but heard her sing!*

[Con moto M. M. ♩ = 80]

1. Had you but heard her sing! How her sweet soul was moun-ted on the
2. The God of Love's grown wise, Has found a new way, how for to sur-

wing, As if 'twould vie with the ce - les - tial sphere.
-prise By Mu - sic's power And us his vas - sals make.

A - pol - lo's Del - phic lyre_____ Could nev - er thus have set_____ my
For where be - fore he took_____ Some few with a be - tray - ing

soul    on fire,        Nor's har-mo-ny have    so be-witched mine ear.
smile   or look,        Thus in an hour he'll    thou-sand cap - tives take.

Had you but heard her sing!
How her sweet soul was mounted on the wing,
As if t'would vie with the celestial sphere.
Apollo's Delphic lyre
Could never thus have set my soul on fire,
Nor 's harmony have so bewitched mine ear.

The God of Love's grown wise,
Has found a new way, how for to surprise
By Music's power
And us his vassals make.
For where before he took
Some few with a betraying smile or look,
Thus in an hour he'll thousand captives take.

## 39 · W. LAWES,

*Gather your rose buds*

Gather your rose buds while you may,
Old Time is still a-flying;
And that same flow'r that smiles today,
Tomorrow will be dying.

The glorious lamp of heaven, the sun,
The higher he is getting,
The sooner will his race be run,
And nearer he's to setting.

That age is best that is the first,
While youth and blood are warmer;
Expect not the last and worst,
Time still succeeds the former.

Then be not coy, but use your time,
While you may, go marry,
For having once but lost your prime,
You may for ever tarry.

*Robert Herrick*

## 40 · NICHOLAS LANIER(E), II (1588–1666),

*The Marigold*

Courts the a-mo-rous Ma-ri-gold, With sigh-ing Blush, and weep-ing
If si-lent tears and sighs dis-co ver Thy grief, thou ne-ver shalt en-

Rain, Yet she re-fu-ses to un-fold. But when the Pla - net
-joy The just re-ward of a bold Lo-ver. But when with mov-ing

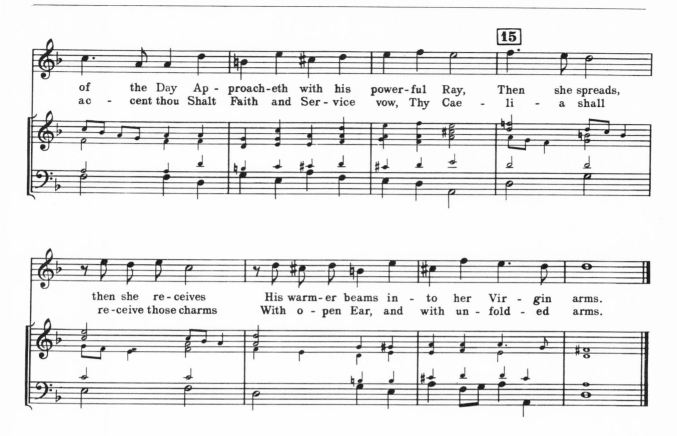

of the Day Ap - proach-eth with his power-ful Ray, Then she spreads,
ac - cent thou Shalt Faith and Ser - vice vow, Thy Cae - li - a shall

then she re - ceives His warm - er beams in - to her Vir - gin arms.
re - ceive those charms With o - pen Ear, and with un - fold - ed arms.

1. Mark how the blushful morn in vain
   Courts the amorous Marigold,
   With sighing Blush, and weeping Rain,
   Yet she refuses to unfold.
   But when the Planet of the Day
   Approacheth with his powerful Ray,
   Then she spreads, then she receives
   His warmer beams into her Virgin arms.

2. So may'st thou thrive in Love, fond Boy,
   If silent tears and sighs discover
   Thy grief, thou never shalt enjoy
   The just reward of a bold Lover.
   But when with moving accent thou
   Shalt constant Faith and Service vow,
   Thy Caelia shall receive those charms
   With open Ear, and with unfolded Arms.

## 41 · LANIER(E),

*Love's Constancy*

[Andante con moto]

1. No more shall Meads___ be deck'd with flowers, nor sweet-ness dwell in
2. Love shall his Bow___ and Shafts lay by, And Ve - nus Doves want

Ro - sie bowers; Nor green-est Buds on___ branch - es spring, nor warb-ling
wings to fly: The Sun re-fuse to___ show___ his Light, and Day shall

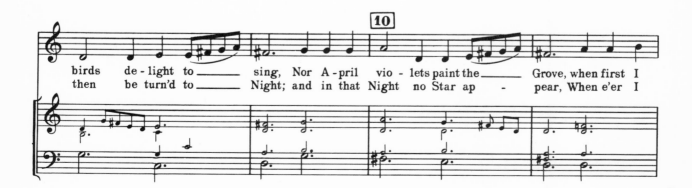

birds de-light to___ sing, Nor A-pril vio-lets paint the___ Grove, when first I
then be turn'd to___ Night; and in that Night no Star ap - pear, When e'er I

No more shall meads be deck'd with flowers,
nor sweetness dwell in Rosie bowers;
Nor greenest Buds on branches spring,
nor warbling birds delight to sing,
Nor April violets paint the Grove,
When first I leave my Celia's love,
when first I leave my Celia's love.

Fishes shall in the Ocean burn,
and Rivers sweet shall bitter turn;
The Humble vale no floods shall know,
though floods shall highest hills o'erflow:
Black Lethe shall Oblivion leave,
when first my Celia I deceive,
whene'er my Celia I deceive.

2. Love shall his Bow and Shafts lay by,
And Venus Doves want wings to fly:
The Sun refuse to show his Light,
and Day shall then be turn'd to Night;
and in that Night no Star appear,
Whene'er I leave my Celia dear.
Love shall no more inhabit Earth,
nor Lovers more shall love for Worth;
nor Joy above in Heaven dwell,
nor pain torment poor Souls in hell;
Grim Death no more shall horrid prove,
Whene'er I leave bright Celia's love.

42 · JOHN BLOW (1649–1708),

*The Self-Banished*

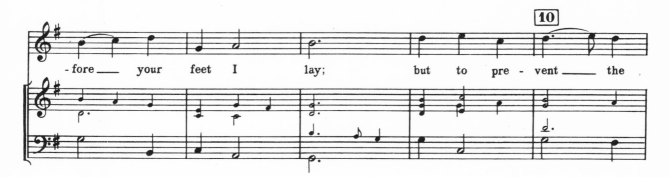

It is not that I love you less
    than when before your feet I lay;
but to prevent the sad increase
    of hopeless love, I keep away:
In vain (alas) for ev'rything,
    which I have known belong to you,
your form does to my fancy bring,
    and makes my old wounds bleed anew.

*Edmund Waller*

43 · BLOW,

*Loving above himself*

stars___will of - ten blame    With all the pas - - - sion of the mind and___

tongue;    Com-plain - ing_words, com - plain - ing_words and notes

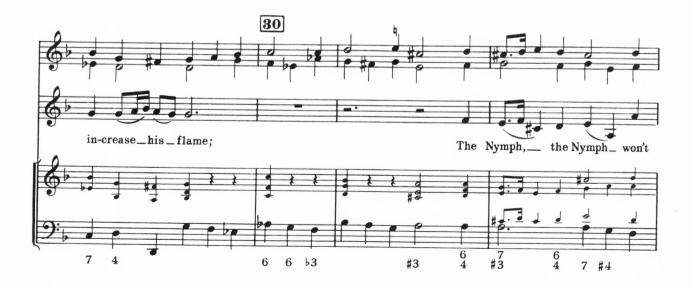

in-crease_his_flame;    The Nymph,___ the Nymph_ won't

Poor Celadon, he sighs, and sighs in vain;
The fair Eugenia must not love,
Nor has a shepherd reason to complain
When tow'ring thoughts his ruin prove.
But Celadon his stars will often blame
With all the passion of the mind and tongue;
Complaining words and notes increase his flame;
The Nymph won't see it but commends the song.
Alas, 'tis plain what causes still his Fate:
What can a verse or note avail?
Birth, Fortune, are as hills of greatest height—
They overlook a lowly, lowly Dale.

## 44 · HENRY PURCELL  (1659–1695),

*Music for awhile*  [z. 583(2)]

eas'd,— eas'd,— eas'd— and dis-dain-ing to be pleas'd till A - lec - to free—— the—

dead, till A-lec - to free the dead from their e - ter - - -

- nal, e-ter - - - - - nal band; Till the snakes drop,

drop, drop, drop, drop, drop, drop, drop, drop from —— her— head, and the

Music for awhile, shall all your cares beguile;
wond'ring how your pains were eas'd
and disdaining to be pleas'd
till Alecto free the dead
from their eternal band;
Till the snakes drop from her head,
and the whip from out her hand.
Music for awhile shall all your cares beguile.

## 45 · PURCELL,

*Winter's Song* [z. 629(32b)]

trem - bling   with   age   And   thus   qui - - - - - v'ring   with

cold;_____   Be - numb'd   with   hard   frost   And   with

sun   to   re - store him,  And   sings _____   as   be - fore.

Next, Winter comes slowly,
Pale, meager and old,
Thus trembling with age
And thus quiv'ring with cold;
Benumb'd with hard frost
And with snow covered o'er;
Prays the sun to restore him,
And sings as before.

### 46 · PURCELL,

*Sweeter than Roses* [z. 585(I)]

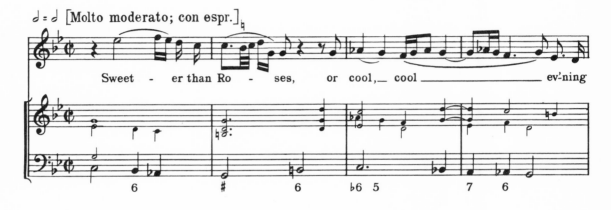

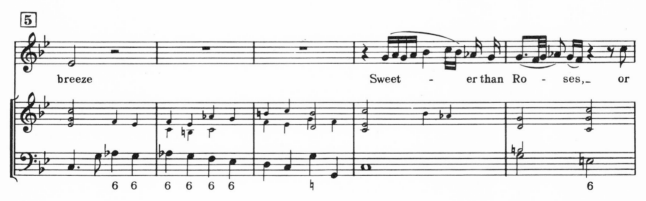

shore, was the dear,\_\_\_\_ the dear,\_\_\_\_ the dear,\_\_\_\_ dear,\_\_\_ dear_____ Kiss;

First, trem - - bling, first, trem - bling, made me,

made me freeze,_____ made me freeze; then shot like fire all,

all, all, all o'er, then shot like fire all, all, all o'er, then shot like fire_____ all, all o'er.

-  -  -  -  -  -  -  -  -  -  -  -  rious _ Love, for

all,        all,     all I touch, all,    all,        all,     all I touch   or   see,   since

that dear, _____     dear _____ Kiss    I    hour-ly, hour - ly __ prove   all, all, all,

all  is Love,       all,  all, all, all, all, all  is Love,   all, all, all, all,   all  is Love, _____

all, all, all, all, all is Love,_____ is Love   to   me.

Sweeter than Roses, or cool ev'ning breeze
on a warm flow'ry shore, was the dear Kiss;
First, trembling, made me freeze;
then shot like fire all o'er.

What magic has victorious Love,
for all I touch or see, since that dear Kiss,
I hourly prove all, all is Love to me.

PART III

# Songs by French Composers

## 47 · GABRIEL BATAILLE (1574–1630),

*Eau vive, source d'amour*

Eau vi - ve sour - ce d'a - mour, de mon ar - deur,

Nin - fe, ra - fraî - chis la vi - o - len - te cha - leur.

Nin - fe, je brû - le d'ai - mer.

La fon - tai - ne sourd ne t'é - clai - re tou - jours: Et la vû - ë la perce et dé -

cou - vre le fond; Rien de ca - ché ____ n'y ver - ras.

Eau vi - ve, mais je ne vois le fond ____ de ton coeur.

| | |
|---|---|
| Eau vive, source d'amour, de mon ardeur, | Living water! Spring of Love, |
| Ninfe, rafraîchis la violente chaleur, | Oh Nymph, cool the violent heat of my desire; |
| Ninfe, je brûle d'aimer. | Nymph! I am burning with love. |
| La fontaine sourd ne t'éclaire toujours: | The silent spring shines always brightly. |
| Et la vûë la perce et découvre le fons; | The eye pierces it and reveals its depths, |
| Rien de caché n'y verras | but you will see nothing hidden there. |
| Eau vive, mais je ne vois le font de ton coeur. | Living water, I cannot see in the depths of your heart. |
| | |
| La fraîche liqueur bel' et claire coulant, | The cool liquid, flowing free and clear, |
| Secourable guérit et soulage la soif | heals and assuages the thirst |
| Au pélerin travaillé; | of the weary pilgrim but, |
| Eau vive, mais tu ne veux ma soif étancher. | Living water, you will not cure my thirst. |
|     Eau vive, source d'amour . . . |     Living water, Spring of love . . . |
| | |
| Quand l'herbe se meurt desséché du soleil, | When the grass dies, dried up by the sun, |
| Quelque pluië de ciel desur-elle venant, | a rain from the skies, falling upon it |
| Gaye, la fair reverdir; | makes it gay and green once more. |
| Eau vive, rends sa vigueur au coeur alangui. | Living water, give the languishing heart new vigor. |
|     Eau vive, source d'amour . . . |     Living water, Spring of love . . . |
| | |
| Un sourjon aval de la roche courant, | A water spring flowing out from under a rock |
| De son onde qui flü et jamais ne tarît, | with its streams running and never stopping, goes on forever; |
| Mène le cours pérannel; | |
| Eau vive, nostr' amour ainsi soit éternel. | Living water, may our love also last forever. |
|     Eau vive, source d'amour . . . |     Living water, Spring of love . . . |
|          *A. de Baïf* | |

### 48 · BATAILLE,

*Qui veut chasser une migraine*

1.

Qui veut chasser une migraine
N'a qu'à boire toujours du bon,
Et maintenir la table pleine
De cervelas et de jambon.
L'eau ne fait rien que pourrir le poumon,
Boute, boute, boute, boute compagnons,
Vuide-nous ce verre et nous le remplirons!

The man who wants to get rid of a headache has only to drink good wine and keep his table loaded with sausage and ham. Water only rots away the lungs. Drink, drink, drink, drink, my hearties! Empty this glass and we will fill it up!

2.

Le vin goûté par ce bon père
Qui s'en rendit si beau garçon,
Nous fait discourir sans grammaire,
Et nous rend savants sans leçon.
      L'eau ne fait . . .

Wine, enjoyed by our worthy father, which makes him such a handsome fellow, makes us talk without learning grammar and makes us clever without education.
      Water only . . .

3.

Loth beuvant dans une caverne
De ses filles enfla le sein,
Montrant qu'un syrop de taverne
Passe celui d'un médecin.
      L'eau ne fait . . .

Lot, drunk in a cave, made his daughters pregnant, demonstrating that the elixir of the tavern is better than that of a doctor.
      Water only . . .

4.

Beuvons donc tous à la bonne heure
Pour nous émouvoir le rognon,
Et que celui d'entre nous meure
Qui dédira son compagnon.
      L'eau ne fait . . .

Let us drink then right away to make our kidneys function, and may the one among us die who says evil of any comrade.
      Water only . . .

## 49 · PIERRE GUÉDRON (1565–ca. 1621),

*C'en est fait, je ne verray*

C'en est fait, je ne ver-rai plus L'a-stre ___

___ que _ la _ mort a re - clus Sous u - ne dure et froi - de la - me,

Pour rendre un tom-beau ___ glo - ri - eux Et ___ rem - plir de dou-leurs mon ___

â - me, La mort en _____ a pri - vé mes yeux.

C'en est fait, je ne verray plus
L'astre que la mort a reclus
Sous une dure et froide lame,
Pour rendre un tombeau glorieux
Et remplir de douleurs mon âme,
La mort en a privé mes yeux.

Ce bel astre ornement des rois
Dont la France observoit les lois,
Heureuse en un si doux empire,
Maintenant honore un cercueil,
Afin que mon coeur qui soupire
Soit à jamais comblé de deuil.

Me faut-il résoudre à ce point
De vivre et de ne le voir point,
Lui qui fut ma gloire et ma vie.
Le soin des choses d'ici bas
Me pourrait-il ôter l'envie
De l'accompagner au trepas?

Non, non, banissant tout plaisir
Je n'aurai plus d'autre désir
Que de le revoir et le suivre,
Et si je vis en ce tourment
C'est mon malheur qui me fait vivre
Pour mes ennuis tant seulement.

Mais j'ai l'esprit insensé
De croire ayant le coeur blessé
Et l'âme encor' m'étant ravie,
Que je sois vive en ce malheur;
Hélas! je suis morte à la vie,
Mais je suis vive à la douleur.

Alceste ainsi reine des coeurs
Soupirait les fieres rigueurs
Dont son infortune l'outrage
Quand elle ouit une voix des cieux,
Qui par le son d'un doux langage
Essuya les pleurs de ses yeux.

It's all ended. I shall never again see that star which Death has buried under a hard, cold slab to make a glorious tomb and fill my soul with grief. Death has deprived my eyes of the sight of him.

This fine star, ornament of kings whose laws France observed, happy under such a rule, now does honor to a tomb; and my grieving heart is forever filled with mourning.

Must I resign myself to living and not seeing him, he who was the glory of my life? Can care for worldly things take from me the desire to accompany him in death?

No! No! giving up every pleasure I shall have no desire but to see him again and follow him. And if I continue to live in torment, it is my sorrow which gives me life.

But my soul is astounded at realizing that, with my heart so wounded and with my very soul taken from me, I can still live in this sorrow. Alas, I am dead to life but I am alive to pain.

Alcestis, queen of our hearts, in the same way, was mourning her suffering from the misfortunes inflicted upon her, when she heard a voice from heaven, which with sweet-sounding speech dried her tears!

## 50 · JOACHIM THIBAUT DE COURVILLE (fl. c. 1570),

*Si je languis d'un martire*

trans - por - - - - te,_____ Me__ dois

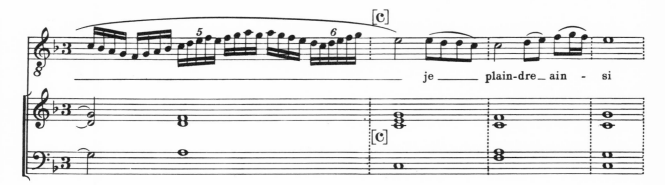

je _____ plain-dre_ain - si

com-me _____ je _____ fais? Un nou - veau __ mal fait _____ de

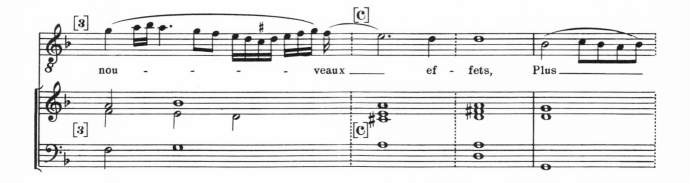

nou - - - - veaux _____ ef - fets, Plus _____

de beau - té     plus de ___ tour - ment ___ ap - por -

- - - - - - - - - - - te.

Si je languis d'un martire incogneu,
Si mon désir jadis tant retenu,
Ores sans bride à son gré me transporte,
Me dois-je plaindre ainsi comme je fais?
Un nouveau mal fait de nouveaux effets,
Plus de beauté plus de tourment apporte.

En ma douleur c'est pour me consoler
Que j'ai osé si hautement voler,
Et que la peur mon courage ne change.
Par les hazards l'honneur se doit chercher.
Quand le malheur me fera trébucher,
L'avoir osé m'est assez de louange.

L'homme grossier en la terre arrêté,
Me peut nommer plein de témérité,
J'aime trop mieux être vue téméraire
Que de coeur lâche et d'esprit abattu.
Un seul sentier n'est clos à la vertu,
Et au couard rien n'est facile à faire.

Les grands palais sont plus battus de vents,
Et les hauts monts vers le ciel s'élevants
Presque toujours sont frappés de l'orage.
Mais c'est tout un: du ciel nous approchant
Cherchons la mort, plutôt qu'en nous cachant
Vivre et montrer qu'ayons peu de courage.

If I am wasting away from an unknown sickness, and my desire, formerly held in check, now carries me away without any hindrance, should I complain as I am now doing? A new evil has different effects, more beauty causes more suffering.

It consoles me in my pain that I have dared to fly so high, and that fear has not affected my courage. Honor should be sought in dangers. When unhappiness makes me waver, it is praise enough for me that I dared aspire.

Though common men, earth-bound, might call me over-bold, I would rather be regarded as too bold than faint-hearted and discouraged. Not one path is closed to the strong, but for the coward nothing is easy.

The great palaces are more buffeted by winds, the high mountains rising toward the sky are nearly always stricken by the storms. But it matters not; let us seek death by approaching the heavens rather than by living hidden away and showing that we have no courage.

## 51 · SEBASTIEN LE CAMUS (c. 1610–1677),

*Amour, cruel Amour*

A - mour, cru-el A - mour, cru-el A - mour, lais-se fi-

-nir mes lar - mes. Je ne sau - rais suf - fire à— tant — d'en-nuis — se -

-crets. Tes sen - si - bles dou - leurs     n'ont pour moi     plus     de char -

- mes.     Faut - il pour un in - grat   de   si   ten - dres re - grets?

A - mour, cru - el  A - mour, cru - el  A - mour,  lais - se fi - nir  mes lar -

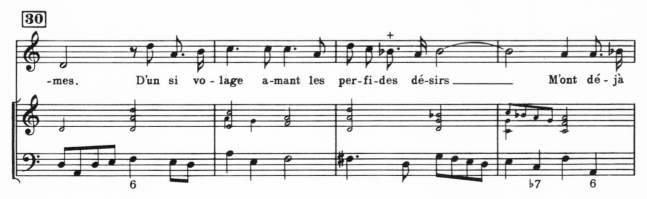

- mes.     D'un si vo - lage  a - mant les per - fi - des dé - sirs _____     M'ont dé - jà

Amour, cruel Amour, laisse finir mes larmes.
Je ne saurais suffire à tant d'ennuis secrets.
Tes sensibles douleurs n'ont pour moi plus de
    charmes.
Faut-il pour un ingrat de si tendres regrets?
Amour, cruel Amour, laisse finir mes larmes.
D'un si volage amant les perfides désirs
M'ont déjà coûté de pleurs et de soupirs,
De mortelles langueurs et de tristes allarmes.
Hélas, pour un ingrat qui ne sait point aimer
Faut-il dans la douleur se perdre et s'abîmer?
Amour, cruel Amour, laisse finir mes larmes.

Love, cruel Love, let my weeping end. I could not
endure such torments in secret. Your tender sorrows have no more charms for me; should I feel
such regrets for an ingrate? Cruel love . . . etc.
Deceitful desires for an unfaithful lover have cost
me too many tears and sighs, mortal anguish and
annoyance. Alas, must I plunge myself in sorrow
and pain for an ingrate who never can love? Cruel
love . . . etc.

## 52 · MICHEL LAMBERT (1610–1696),

*Vous ne sauriez, mes yeux*

Vous ne sau - riez, mes yeux, ré - pan - dre ré - pan - dre trop de lar - mes; I- -ris, l'in-grate, I-ris me dé-fend de la voir. Mon coeur l'a-vait pré- -vu par ses tri - - - stes al - lar - mes Dans l'ex-

-cès  de mon dés - es - poir.          Vous      ne    sau - riez, mes yeux,          ré - pan -

-dre,          ré - pan - dre    trop  de  lar - mes.

C'est   par    vous    que j'ai

vu     les   char - mes  De  l'in - gra - te  qui m'a chan -

Vous ne sauriez, mes yeux, répandre trop de
  larmes;
Iris, l'ingrate, Iris me défend de la voir.
Mon coeur l'avait prévu par ses tristes allarmes
Dans l'excès de mon désespoir.

Vous ne sauriez, mes yeux, répandre trop de
  larmes.

C'est par vous que j'ai vu les charmes
De l'ingrate qui m'a changé.
C'est vous, hélas, c'est vous qui m'avez engagé.

Vous ne sauriez, mes yeux, répandre trop de
  larmes.

Oh eyes of mine, you could not shed enough
tears! Iris, the wretch, forbids me to see her. My
heart had foreseen it and was alarmed, when I
was attacked by despair.

My eyes, you could not shed tears enough!

It was through you, my eyes, that I first perceived
the charms of the woman who has changed me; it
was you, alas, who got me so involved.

You could not shed enough tears, oh eyes of mine!

## 53 · JEAN-BAPTISTE LULLY (1632–1687),

*Plainte de Vénus sur la mort d'Adonis*

Ah,____ quel - le cru-au - té de ne pou-voir_____ mou-

- rir  Et  d'a - voir  un __ coeur tendre  et  for - mé  pour souf - frir.

Ah,        Ah! ____                quel - le cru-au - té        de ne

pou-voir____ mou-rir.

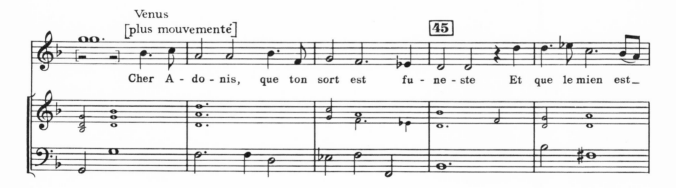

Et n'en fait pas à moi-tié! Que les traits de la mort au-roient pour moi des char-mes,

Mais sur mes jours ils n'ont point __ de pou-voir, Et ma di-vi-ni-té ré-

-duit mon dés-es-poir À d'é-ter - nels sou-pirs, à d'é-ter-nel - les lar - mes.

Et ma di-vi - ni - té ré-duit mon dés-es-poir ré-duit mon dés-es-poir à d'é-ter-nels sou-

Ah, quelle cruauté de ne pouvoir mourir
Et d'avoir un coeur tendre et formé pour souffrir.
Cher Adonis, que ton sort est funeste
Et que le mien est digne de pitié;
Viens monstre furieux, viens dévorer le reste
Et n'en fait pas à moitié!
Que les traits de la mort auroient pour moi des charmes,
Mais pur mes jours ils n'ont point de pouvoir,
Et ma divinité reduit mon désespoir
A d'éternels soupirs, à d'éternelles larmes.

Ah, how cruel not to be able to die, to have a tender heart destined to suffer! Adorable Adonis, how terrible is your fate and how worthy mine is of pity! Come, fierce monster, come devour the rest, and not merely half of it! What charm the countenances of Death would have for me, but now it has no power over my fate; and my divine nature reduces my despair to eternal sighing and weeping!

## 54 · MARC-ANTOINE CHARPENTIER (1654–1704),

*Pour l'Élevation*

Panis angelicus fit panis hominum, dat panis coelicum figuris terminum. O res mirabilis, manducat Dominum pauper, servus, et humilis.

The bread of Angels becomes the bread of Man; the bread gives divine purpose to its form. Oh miracle! The poor, the servant, the humble partake of Our Lord.

## 55 · JEAN-BAPTISTE MOREAU (1656–1733),

*Cantique. Sur les vaines occupations*
*des gens du Siècle*

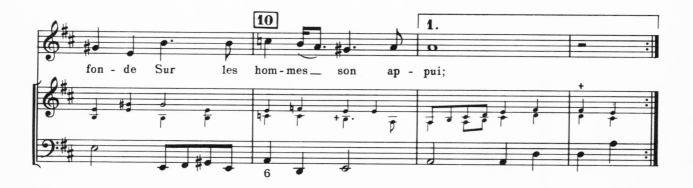

- pui;  Leur gloi-re fuit, et s'ef-fa-ce  En moins de

6#

temps que la tra-ce Du vais-seau ___ qui ___ fend les mers,  Ou de la flè  -  che ra-

-pi - de, Qui loin de l'oeil qui la gui-de  Cher-che l'oi-seau _____ dans _____ les

airs.  airs.

Choeur [a l'unisson]

De la Sa-gesse im-mor-tel - le La voix tonne et nous in - struit;

En - fants des hom-mes, dit - el - le,     De vos soins quel est     le     fruit?

[Seule]

Par quelle er-reur, â - mes vai-nes, Du plus pur sang de vos vei - nes A-che-tez-vous si sou-

- vent,         Non un     pain     qui vous re-pais - se, Mais un     om - bre qui vous

lais-se Plus af - fa - mez que de-vant, Plus af - fa - mez que de-vant.

[Choeur]

Le pain que je vous pro-po - se Sert aux An - ges d'a-li-

-ment: Dieu lui - mê - me le com - po - se De la fleur de son fro-

1. 2.

-ment. Le -ment. C'est ce pain si dé - lec - ta - ble Que ne sert

point à sa ta-ble Le mon - de que vous sui - vez; Je l'offre à qui me veut

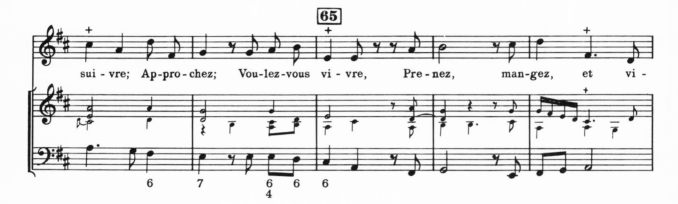

sui - vre; Ap-pro-chez; Vou-lez-vous vi - vre, Pre - nez, man-gez, et vi -

- vez.          Pre - nez,          man - gez, _____ et vi - vez.

O __ Sa-ges-se! ta __ pa-ro-

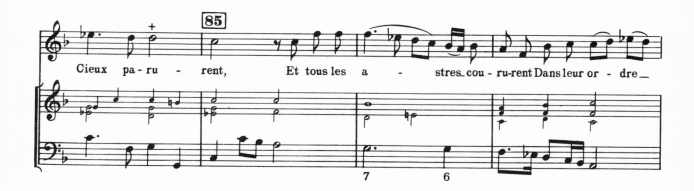

rè - gnes;     Et qui suis - je que tu dai - gnes Jus-qu'à moi ___ te ra - bais-ser? ___

A - vant les

Le verbe, i - ma - ge du Pè - re, Lais - sa son trône é - ter - nel,     Et

d'u - ne mor-tel – le Mè - re Vou-lut naî-tre homme et mor-tel: Com-me l'or-

- gueil fut – le cri - me Dont il nais-soit la – vic - ti - me, Il de-poüil-

-la — sa splen-deur, Et vint pauvre et mi-se - ra - ble, Ap-prendre à l'hom-me cou-

-pa - ble Sa ve-ri - ta - ble – gran - deur, Sa ve-ri - ta - ble gran-deur.

Quel charme vainqueur du monde
Vers Dieu m'élève aujourd'hui,
Malheureux l'homme qui fonde
Sur les hommes son appui;
Leur gloire fuit, et s'efface
En moins de temps que la trace
Du vaisseau qui fend les mers,
Ou de la flèche rapide,
Qui loin de l'oeil qui la guide
Cherche l'oiseau dans les airs.

What overpowering spell raises me today from the world towards God? Wretched is the man who bases his hopes upon his fellow man! Their glory fades and disappears in less time than the traces of a vessel on the ocean, or the swift arrow which, far from its guiding eye, strikes the bird in the air.

De la Sagesse immortelle
La voix tonne et nous instruit;
Enfants des hommes, dit-elle,
De vos soins quel est le fruit?
Par quelle erreur, âmes vaines,
Du plus pur sang de vos veines
Achetez-vous si souvent,
Non un pain qui vous repaise,
Mais un ombre qui vous laisse
Plus affamez que devant.
Le pain que je vous propose
Sert aux Anges d'aliment:
Dieu lui-même le compose
De la fleur de son froment.
C'est ce pain si délectable
Que ne sert point à sa table
Le monde que vous suivez;
Je l'offre à qui me veut suivre;
Approchez; Voulez-vous vivre,
Prenez, mangez, et vivre.

O Sagesse! ta parole
Fit éclore l'Univers,
Posa sur un double pole
La terre au milieu des mers:
Tu dis, et les Cieux parurent,
Et tous les astres coururent
Dans leur ordre se placer:
Avant les siècles tu règnes;
Et qui suis-je que tu daignes
Jusqu'à moi te rabaisser?
Le verbe, image du Père,
Laissa son trône éternel,
Et d'une mortelle Mère
Voulut naître homme, et mortel;
Comme l'orgueil fut le crime
Dont il naissoit la victime,
Il depoüilla sa splendeur,
Et vint pauvre et miserable,
Apprendre à l'homme coupable
Sa veritable grandeur.
L'âme heureusement captive
Sous son joug trouve la paix,
Et s'abreuve d'une eau vive
Qui ne s'épuise jamais;
Chacun peut boire en cette onde,
Elle invite tout le monde.
Mais nous courons follement
Chercher des sources bourbeuses,
Ou des citernes trompeuses,
D'où l'eau fuit à tout moment.

*Jean Racine*

The voice of immortal Wisdom thunders and tells us: "Children of Man," it says, "what is the fruit of all your strivings? By what error do you so often buy with the blood from your veins, not bread to nourish you, but a mere shadow, which leaves you hungrier than ever? The bread which I offer you is the food of angels, God himself makes it from his best wheat. It is delectable bread I offer you, which the world does not serve´at its table. I offer it to anyone who is willing to follow me. Come! Do you wish to live fully? Take some, eat it and live."

Oh Wisdom, your voice made the universe burst into blossom; placed the earth on its double axis amid the seas: you spoke and the stars hastened to place themselves in their right places. You have reigned since before the beginning of time, and what am I that you should deign to come down to me? The Word, image of the Father, left his eternal throne and, born of a mortal mother, wished to become man and mortal. Since Pride was the sin whose victim he became, he doffed his splendor and came, poor and wretched, to teach sinful man his real greatness.

The Soul, a willing captive, finds peace under your control and drinks deep of a living water which can never be exhausted. All can drink of this flood; the whole world is invited, but we wildly search out the muddy springs or the deceptive wells from which the water eternally escapes.

## 56 · SEBASTIEN DE BROSSARD (1655–1730),

Motet. *Qui non diligit Te*

**Affettuoso**

Qui non di - li - git Te non a - - - - mat

Te, O dul - cis, dul - cis, dul - cis a - mor! Ô,

ô,   ô_____   dul - cis a - - mor!   [Vln. I + II

Qui non di - li-git Te,       [Vln.   ]        Qui non

di - li-git Te, Ô dul - cis___ a - mor! Non non,   non

non,     non a - mat, non non,    non a - mat Te.    Non

[Vlns.

a - - - - - mat,     non  a - mat,  non  a - mat

Te.
[Vlns. + B. C.

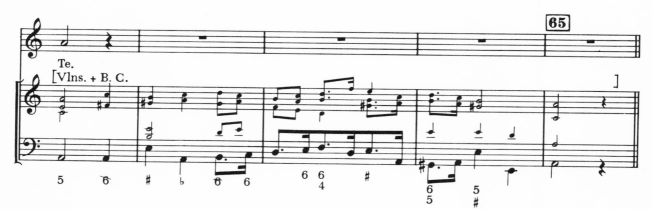

Largo

Tu so - la,   tu  so-la es a  mun-da pul-chri-tu   -   do,  Tu ve-ra es, tu

ve - ra  a - ni-ma be-a-ti - tu-do;    An - ge-lo-rum et ho - mi-num,  Tu pe-

-ren - nes de-li - ci - a, pe-ren ─ ─ ─ ─ nes de-li - ci -

**Allegro**

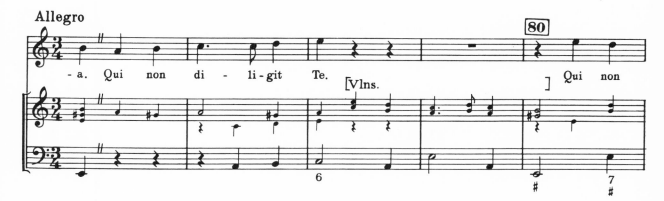

-a. Qui non di - li - git Te. [Vlns.] Qui non

di ─ ─ ─ ─ ─ ─ ─ ─ li - git

Te non a - mat, non a - mat Te, non a ─ ─ ─

Aria 1ª

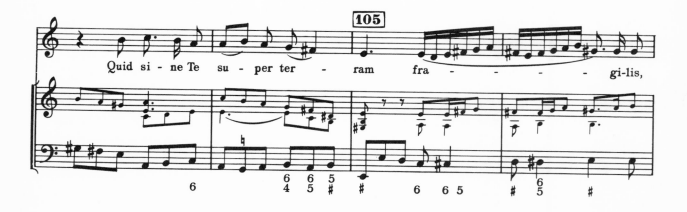

fra - - - - gi-lis,___ ve-nu - stas, fal-lax sem - - -

- per, fal - lax sem-per, vo-lup-tas, va - le - te, va-le - te, va - le - te, va-le -

- te?     Ca - du - ca ___ mun - di ___

**Aria 2ª**

gau - di - a,     Ca - du - ca ___ mun - di ___ gau - - di - a mor-

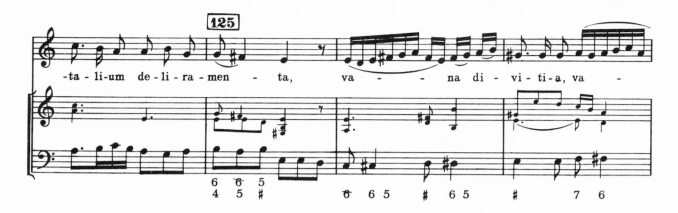

-ta-li-um de-li-ra-men — ta, va — — na di-vi-ti-a, va —

- — — — na — di-vi-ti-a. O fal-la — — ces! O fal-

-la-ces! Va-le-te, va-le-te men-da-ces, va-le — — — — te pu-ri-

-o-ri, ac-cen — — — — — — — dor — i —

Largo

De-scen-dat, de-scen-dat er - go, mi Je - su. De-

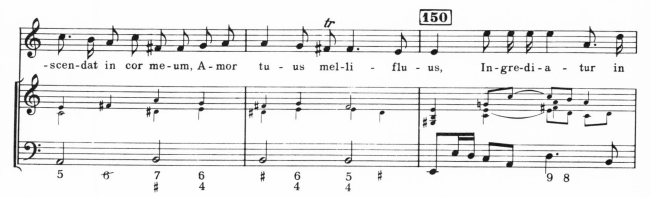

-scen-dat in cor me-um, A-mor tu - us mel-li - flu-us, In-gre-di-a - tur in

i - psum a-mor tu - us per-pe - - - tu-us.

Qui non diligit Te non amat Te,
O dulcis amor!
Tu sola es a munda pulchritudo,
Tu vera es anima beatitudo;
Angelorum et hominum,
Tu perennes delicia.
Quid nobis in coelo?
Quid sine Te super terram
fragilis, venustas, fallex semper,
voluptas valete?
Caduca mundi gaudia mortalium
deliramenta, vana divitia.
O fallaces!
valete mendaces,
valete puriori, accendor igne.
Descendit ergo, mi Jesu.
Descendit in cor meum,
Amor viris mellifluus,
Ingrediatur in ipsum amor tuus perpetuus.

He who does not delight in Thee does not really love Thee, Oh sweet Love! Thou art the beauty of purity, thou art the true blessedness of the soul; of angels and men thou art eternal delight. What is there for us on earth—fragile, vain, always in error—without Thee?

Transitory worldly pleasure of mortal man, vanity, useless wealth, Oh deceit! Thou prevailest over the false, thou prevailest, kindler of purifying fire. Descend, oh my Jesus, descend into my heart; sweet love of mankind, may your perpetual love enter into my heart.

## 57 · CHRISTOPHE BALLARD (fl. c. 1703),

*Brunete*

**[Andante]**

Le beau Ber - ger Tir - cis, Près___ de sa___ chère An - ne - te:

Second Couplet

Ah! pe - tit à pe - tit, Je___ sens que je m'en - ga - ge

Autres Couplets

Le sou - ci___jau - nis - sant, La pâ - le_Vi - o - let - te:

6 6 #

Ornaments:

+ = Cadence precipitée   or

∧ = Port de voix feint    or   =

∨ = Port de voix entier   or   =

-ne - te, Ah!_____ tu me fais mou - rir!

sa - ge, Mes_____ yeux___ en _ ont ___ trop dit.

-ne - te, Ah!_____ tu _ me___ fais___ mou - rir!

Le beau Berger Tircis,
Près de sa chère Annete:
Sur les bords du Loire assis,
Chantait dessus sa Musete:
Ah! petite Brunete,
Ah tu me fais mourir!

Ah! petit à petit,
Je sens que je m'engage:
L'Amour prend trop de crédit,
Je n'en dis pas davantage,
Ma bouche soyez sage,
Mes yeux en ont trop dit.

Le souci jaunissant,
La pâle violette:
Sont les fleurs que vont naissant
Des larmes que Tircis jette;
Ah! petite Brunete,
Ah! tu me fais mourir!

The handsome shepherd Tircis, seated on the banks of the Loire near his dear Annette, sang to his Musette: Ah! little Brunete, Ah you make me suffer!

Ah, little by little I feel myself ensnared: Love is too strong. I will say no more—be wise, my mouth; my eyes have already said too much.

The yellow marigold, the pale violet, are the flowers that will spring from tears Tircis lets fall; Ah, little Brunete, Ah you make me suffer!

### 58 · MICHEL PINOLET DE MONTÉCLAIR (1667–1737),

*Brunete*

Le beau Ber - ger Tir - cis, Loin de sa chère An - net - te: Sur les

bords du Loire as - sis, Chan - tait des - sus sa Mu - set - te: Ah!

pe - ti - te Bru - ne - te, Ah! ___ tu ___ me fais ___ mou - rir!

Text and translation as in No. 57.

### 59 · FRANÇOIS COUPERIN (1668–1733),

*10ème et 11ème Versets du Motet composé*

*de l'ordre du Roy, 1705*

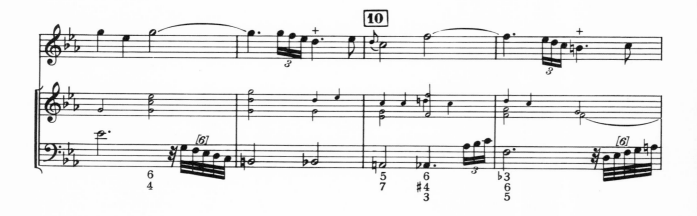

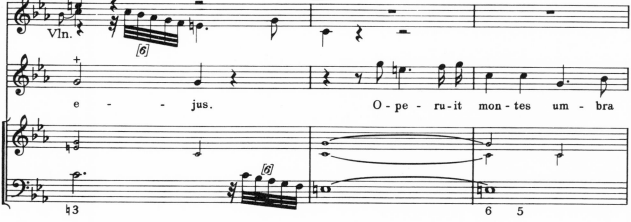

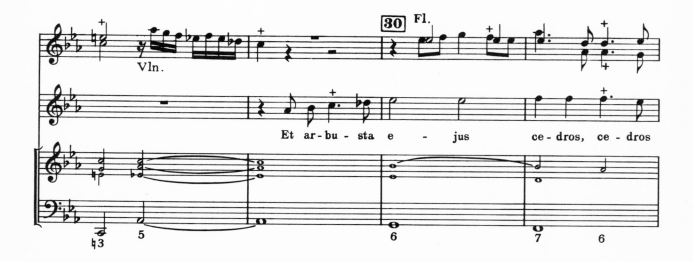

**[Più mosso]**
2ème verset

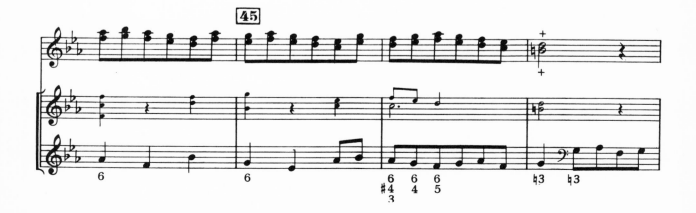

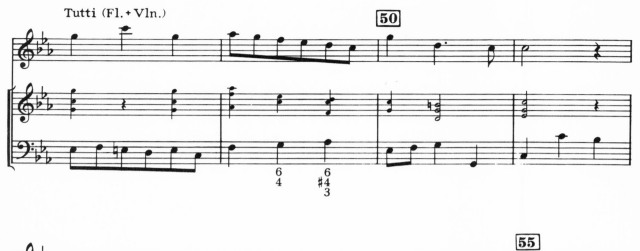

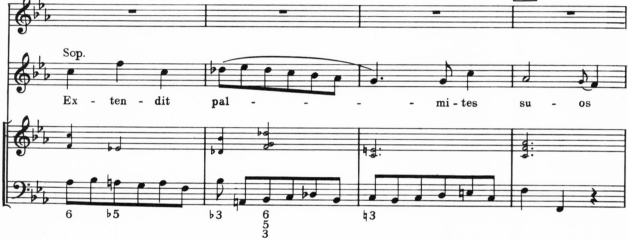

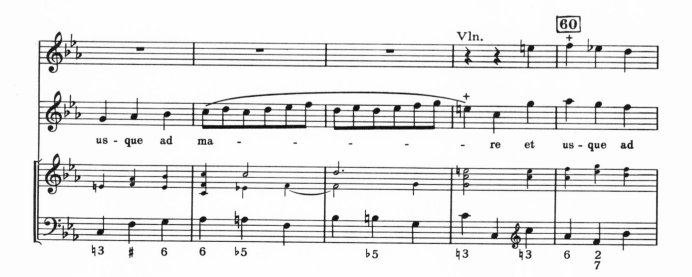

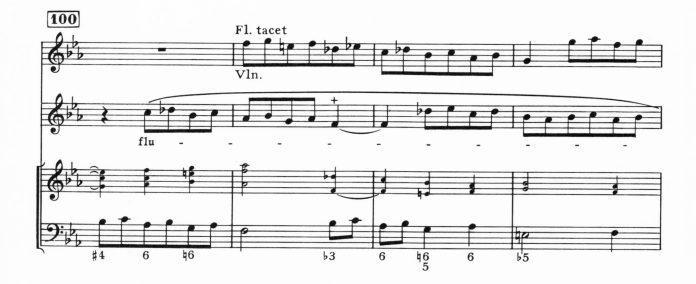

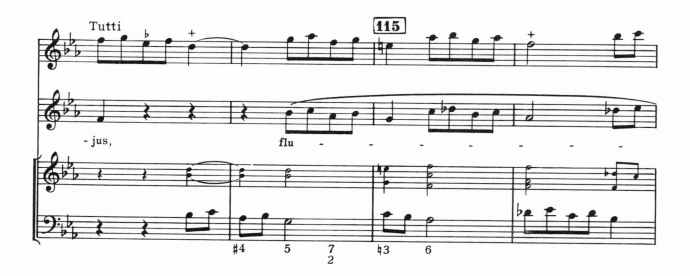

-   -   -   -   men   pro - pa - gi - nes   e   -   jus.

10.

Operuit montes umbra ejus,
Et arbusta ejus cedros Dei.

The hills were covered with the shadow of it (i.e. vine) and the boughs thereof were like the goodly cedar trees.

11.

Extendit palmites suos usque ad mare
et usque ad flumen propagines ejus.

She stretched out her branches unto the sea, and her boughs unto the river.

### 60 · COUPERIN,

*Doux liens.*

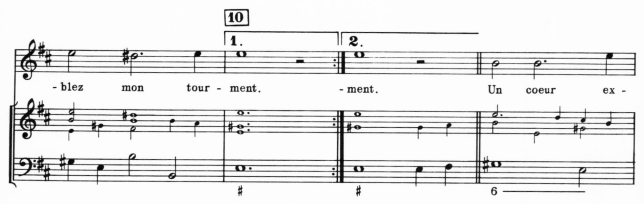

Doux liens de mon coeur,
Aimable peines,
Charmantes chaînes,
De moment en moment
Redoublez mon tourment.
Un coeur exempt de nos tendres allarmes
Ne ressentit jamais que de faibles douçeurs;
C'est dans l'excès de ses rigueurs
Que l'Amour a caché ses plus doux charmes.

Sweet charms of my heart! beloved suffering! charming bonds! increase my torment at every moment. A heart which does not feel love's fears has felt only the smallest pleasure; for it is in his worst suffering that love has hidden his greatest pleasure.

## 61 · LOUIS NICHOLAS CLÉRAMBAULT (1676–1749),

*Monarque redouté* from *Orphée*

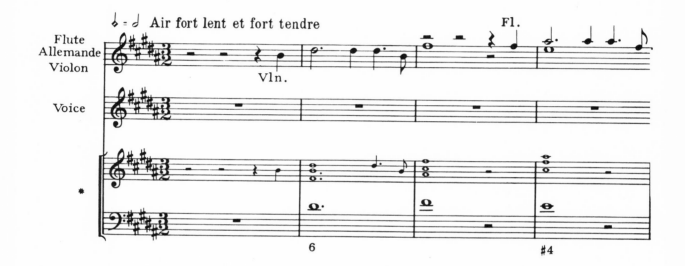

* Marked "Violon et Clavecin."

Mo - nar - que re - dou - té    de ces roy-aum-es som - bres,

Je suis le fils    du Dieu du jour,    Plus mal - heu-reux cent

fois    que vos plus tri - stes om - bres, Et mon mal-heur est cau - sé    par l'a-

-mour.

Vous voy-ez un A-mant fi-dè-le Pri-vé du seul ob-

-jet qui l'a-vait en-flam-mé; Hé-las! le bon-

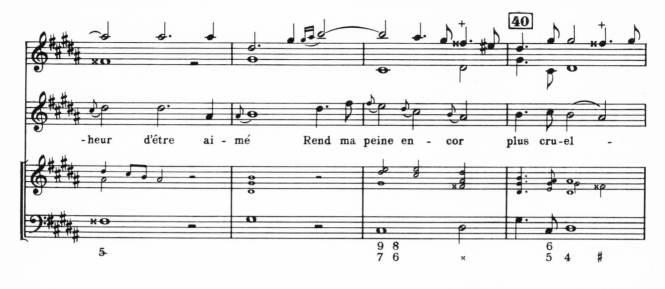

-pri - ce;      Ren - dez-moi  ma chère  Eu-ri-di - ce,

Ne  sé-pa - rez  pas____ nos____ deux coeurs, Ren - dez-moi    ma chère  Eu-ri-

-di - ce,      Ne  sé-pa - rez  pas____ nos____ deux coeurs.

Monarque redouté de ces royaumes sombres,
Je suis le fils du Dieu du jour,
Plus malheureux cent foix que vos plus tristes
   ombres,
Et mon malheur est causé par l'amour.
Vous voyez un Amant fidèle
Privé du seul objet qui l'avait enflammé;
Hélas! le bonheur d'être aimé
Rend ma peine encor plus cruelle!
Laissez-vous toucher par mes pleurs,
D'un sort affreux réparez le caprice;
Ne séparez pas nos coeurs,
Rendez-moi ma chère Euridice.

Mighty Monarch of the dark kingdom, I am the son of the Sun god, a thousand times more unhappy than your saddest shades, and my unhappiness is caused by love. You see before you a faithful lover, deprived of the one creature he ever loved. Alas, the happiness of being loved in return makes my pain all the greater. Be moved by my tears, remedy the caprice of an evil fate; do not separate two hearts, return to me my beloved Euridice.

## 62 · ANDRÉ CAMPRA (1660–1744),

### Two airs from *L'Europe Galant*

Sou - pi - rez jeu - nes coeurs, Sui - vez ce qu'A - mour vous in -

-spi - re. Cent nou - vel - les dou - ceurs Vous at - tend - ent

dans son em - pi - re. Sou - pi - rez, jeu - nes

Ai - mons dans la jeu - ne sai - son, Cé - dons, cé - dons à la

ten - dres - se; Nous en faut - il au - tre rai - son,

Que le pen - chant qui nous em - pres - se?     Ai -

-se?     En     vain un er - reur ex - trê - me     Nous de -

*Air*

| Soupirez jeunes coeurs, | Sigh, young hearts, |
|---|---|
| Suivez ce qu'Amour vous inspire. | Do what love inspires you to; |
| Cent nouvelles douceurs | A hundred new pleasures |
| Vous attendent dans son empire. | Await you in his realm. |
| Soupirez jeunes coeurs, | Sigh, young hearts, |
| Devrait-on vous le dire? | Must you be told what to do? |

*Chorus*

| Aimez, aimez, belle bergère, | Fall in love, beautiful shepherdess, |
|---|---|
| Laissez-vous enflammer: | Let yourself go. |
| Que sert l'avantage de plaire | What good is pleasing without the pleasure |
| Sans le plaisir d'aimer? | Of loving in return? |

*Air*

| Aimons dans la jeune saison, | Let us love in the Springtime, |
|---|---|
| Cédons, cédons à la tendresse; | Let us yield to love! |
| Nous en faut-il autre raison | Do we need any other reason |
| Que le penchant qui nous empresse? | Than our own inclination? |
| En vain un erreur extrême | A great mistake vainly forbids us |
| Nous défend de nous enflammer; | To fall in love, |
| Notre coeur sent assez lui-même | Our heart itself tells us |
| Le besoin qu'il a d'aimer. | Of our need to love. |

# PART IV

# Songs by German Composers

## 63 · THOMAS SELLE (1599–1663),

### *Amarilli, du schönstes Bild*

1. A - ma - ril - li du schön-stes Bild,    mein e - wig's Herz freund -
2. Wann ich dei - ne *di - scre - ti - on*    be-tracht und an - dre

- lich und    mild,    Wann ich an-schau die Son - ne    der hel - le
 __ Tu - gend, schon    tut mir das Her - ze wal - len    für gros-se *af -*

Aüg - lein __ dein, emp-find ich Freud    und Won - ne    im jun - gen
*fet - ti - on,* und hat al - lein    ge - fal - len    an dir meins

Herz - ens __ mein.    Muss tri - on - fi - ren und in - to -
Herz - ens __ Kron.

ni - ren Vi - va, vi - va, vi - va, vi - va

vi - va l'a - mo - re! Vi - va, vi - va,

vi - va, vi - va, vi - va l'a - mo - re!

Amarilli du schönstes Bild,

Mein ewigs Herz, freundlich und mild,

Wann ich anschau die Sonne der helle Äuglein dein,

Empfind ich Freud und Wonne im jungen Herzens mein.

Muss trionfiren und intonieren

Viva, viva, viva, viva, viva l'amore!

Wann ich deine *discretion*

Betracht und andre Tugend, schon

Tut mir das Herze wallen für grosse *affettion,*

Und hat allein gefallen an dir meins Herzens Kron.

Muss trionfiren . . .

Amarillis, pretty as a picture, my true heart, loving and gentle, when I gaze into the light of thy two clear eyes, happiness and joy fill my young heart. I must rejoice and sing "Viva l'amore!"

When I contemplate thy *discretion* and thy other virtues, my heart flutters with *affection* and gives thee alone the crown.

I must rejoice . . .

## 64 · HEINRICH ALBERT (1604–1651),

*Mein liebstes Seelchen*

1. Mein lieb-stes Seel - chen, lasst uns le - ben So lang wir

noch im Le - ben sein! Bald bricht der Schlim - me Tod her -

ein, So müs-sen wir, das ü - ber ge - ben Was uns so

sanft und lin-de tat, Was uns so oft er-göt-zet hat.

Mein liebstes Seelchen lasst uns leben
So lang wie noch im Leben sein!
Bald bricht der Schlimme Tod herein,
So müssen wir das übergeben
Was uns so sanft und linde tat,
Was uns so oft ergötzet hat.

Der Augen umgewechselt Scherzen,
Die Seufzer, die so mancherhand
Durch abgeredeten Verstand
Die Botschaft brachten von dem Herzen,
Vergeh'n und werden gleich zu nicht'
Sobald der Atem uns gebricht.

Drum, weil die Brust sich noch kann heben
Eh' uns der warme Geist entweicht,
Eh' euer Purpurmund verbleicht,
Mein liebstes Seelchen, lasst uns leben!
Geniesset, was die Zeit beschert,
Wer sichert uns wie lang es währt?

*R. Roberthin*

My dearest let us really live as long as we are still alive. Soon dreary Death comes, and we must renounce what was so sweet and lovely to us and gave us pleasure so often.

The continual sparkling of our eyes, the sighs which so often brought messages from the heart in unspoken understanding—these all pass away and become nothing as soon as we no longer breathe.

So while our bosoms can still heave, before this warm feeling escapes us, before your rosy lips grow pale, my dearest, let us really live! Enjoy what Time ruins; who can assure us how long it will last?

## 65 · HEINRICH SCHÜTZ (1585–1672),

*Ich liege und schlafe* [SWV 310]

Denn du schlä-gelst al - le mei-ne Fein-de auf den Bak - ken und zer -

schmet-terst der Gott - lo - sen Zäh - - - - - ne,

und zer-schmet-terst der Gott - lo - sen Zäh - - - - -

ne. Bei dem Her - ren, bei dem Her - ren

fin - det man Hil - fe, fin - det man Hil - fe, fin - det man

Hil - fe,        und dei - nen Se - gen ü - ber dein Volk,

Se - - - - - - - - - la,

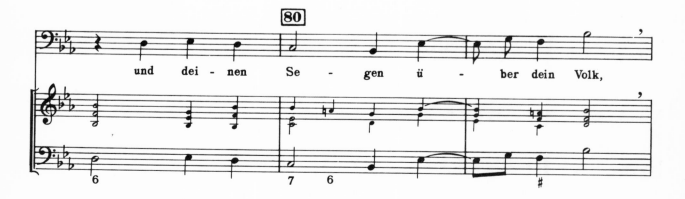

und dei - nen Se - gen ü - ber dein Volk,

Ich liege und schlafe, und erwache, denn der
Herr hält mich.
Ich fürchte mich nicht für viel Hunderttausenden,
die sich umher wider mich legen.

Auf, Herr, und hilf mir, hilf mir mein Gott. Denn
du schlägest alle meine Feinde auf den Bakken
    und
zerschmetterst der Gottlosen Zähne.

Bei dem Herren findet man Hilfe, und deinen
    Segen
über dein Volk. Sela.

I laid me down and slept, and rose up again; for
the Lord sustained me. I will not be afraid for ten
thousands of the people who have set themselves
against me round about.

Up, Lord, and help me, O my God, for thou
smitest all mine enemies upon the cheek-bone;
thou hast broken the teeth of the ungodly.

Salvation belongeth unto the Lord; and thy blessing is upon thy people. Selah.

*Ps. 3:58*

## 66 · ANDREAS HAMMERSCHMIDT (1612–1675),

Sarabande. *Gluckselig Rosilis.*

dass wir ver - lie - bet der Lie - be mehr pfle - gen.

Glückselig Rosilis, mag ich mich schätzen
Dass eure Wangen mich werden ergetzen,
Der hellen Augenglantz der kaum erregen,
Dass wir verliebt der Liebe mehr pflegen.

Dieses thut eure vollkommend Tugend
Das macht die keusche Pracht und schöne Jugend.
Nicht ist die Thyrsis mit schlechten gebehrden,
Dass sie unfreundlich gefunden mag werden.

Pallas zwar giebet sehr weise Gemühter,
Venus gibt schönheit und Juno gibt güter.
Diese drei Stücke Rosilis darreichet.
Drumb Pallas, Venus und Juno ihr weichet.

Demnach des Himmels gunst seligh will machen
Dass ihr Wangen mich freundlich anlachen,
Erfreuet sich mein Sinn zu umfangen
Selbsten Cupido trägt grosser verlangen.

Berg und auch Thäler die springen vor freuden
Schäfer und Schäferin auf grüner Heiden.
Mein Rosilis mich hertzlichen liebet
Welche zur Liebsten sich gantz mir ergiebet.

Lasset ihr Götter und alle Göttinnen
Euer Ton klingen aufs Helicons Zinnen;
Danckbar wird sich die Rosilis bezeigen,
Was sie besitzet mir geben zu eigen.

Fair Rosilis, I think myself lucky that your beautiful face delights me, that your clear eyes inspire me; since we are in love, let us enjoy the pleasures of love.

This is what your perfect virtue does, your maidenly beauty and lovely youth. Not so is Tirsis, with her unseemly behavior, which makes her seem disagreeable.

Pallas indeed bestows wisdom; Venus gives beauty, and Juno worldly goods. These three things Rosilis displays—therefore Pallas, Venus, and Juno yield to her.

So heaven's grace will bless me if her eyes look on me with favor. My heart rejoices to realize even Cupid suffers great desires.

Hills and vales dance with joy, shepherd and shepherdess frolic in the green fields; my Rosilis loves me with all her heart and admits she is my sweetheart.

Gods and Goddesses, let your shouts ring over all Helicon's mountains! Gladly will Rosilis consent to give me what she possesses as my own.

## 67 · ADAM KRIEGER (1634–1666),

*Fleug, Psyche, fleug*

Presto

Und in der Stir - ne blit - zet, Da muss die süs - se Lie - bes-pein Voll Hitz und Feu -

- - - - - - er sein.

Ritornello I

Fine

1. Frei-lich, frei-lich ist die Glut, So da-hier in eu-rem Mut Und in al-len A-dern bren-net,
2. Hier lasst ihr die Lie-bes-flamm Eu-rem lieb-sten Bräu-ti-gam, Gleich nach sei-nem Her-zen schies -
3. So ge-nies-se frisch und frei Dei-ne Lust, du schö-nes zwei, Und er-lan-ge dein Ver-lan -

— Von der Ve-nus an-ge-zünd't, Weil sie, gar zu lie-bes Kind, Gleich nach eu-ren Au-gen ren-net.
-sen. Er hin-ge-gen lacht und denkt, Was ihn itz und heim-lich kränkt, Bald voll-kom-men zu ge-nies-sen.
-gen. Was der Him-mel Gu-tes gibt, Sei in dich zu-gleich ver-liebt, So kannst du ver-gnü-get pran-gen.

*Ritornello II*

hoch - ge - schätz - ten Him - mels - ga - ben     Mit Freu - den kön - nen bei uns ha - ben.

Fleug, Psyche, fleug,
Cupido will nicht mehr dein eigen sein.
Hier hat er sich in diesen hellen Augen
Der Zarten Braut ein Wohnhaus aufgebaut.
Dir, o schönste Zier,
Erwirbt er nur allein dergleichen Ehr
Und schätzt dich gleich der wundervollen Psyche,
Von der er neulich wiche.
Wo nun Cupido sitzet
Und in der Stirne blitzet,
Da muss die süsse Liebespein
Voll Hitz und Feuer sein.

Freilich, freilich ist die Glut,
So dahier in eurem Mut
Und in allen Adern brennet,
Von der Venus angezünd't,
Weil sie, gar zu liebes Kind,
Gleich nach euren Augen rennet.

Hier lasst ihr die Liebesflamm
Eurem liebsten Bräutigam,
Gleich nach seinem Herzen schiessen.
Er hingegen lacht und denkt,
Was ihn itzund heimlich kränkt,
Bald vollkommen zu geniessen.

So geniesse frisch und frei
Deine Lust, du schönes zwei,
Und erlange dein Verlangen,
Was der Himmel Gutes gibt,
Sei in dich zugleich verliebt,
So kannst du vergnüget prangen.

Wir wünschen euch and eurem Herzen
Ein recht erfreulich Liebesscherzen,
Eine Glücke von des Himmels Höhe,
Dass alles Trauern von euch gehe.
Ein süss und angenehmes Lieben,
Das alle Welt, so oft getrieben,
Ein Herz und Sinn und eine Seele
So lange wir in dieser Höhle
Dich hochgeschätzten Himmelsgaben
Mit Freuden können bei uns haben.

Begone, Psyche, begone! Cupid no longer is yours alone, but has built himself a dwelling in the bright eyes of the lovely bride.

Oh my treasure! he grants you the same honor and esteems you just as much as the alluring Psyche, from whom he has just parted.

Where Cupid abides now, and shines from her brow, there must the pains of love be hot and fiery.

Bright is the glow in heart and veins, kindled by Venus, when he, the too-lovely boy, appears in your eyes.

Now in our dear bridegroom's heart blazes the flame of love, and he laughs and thinks that what causes him to suffer now he will soon gladly enjoy.

So enjoy your new pleasures, oh lovely couple and fulfill your hearts' desire. May whatever good things heaven bestows, be fulfilled in you and may you be content.

We wish you delight in love's game, and heavenly happiness. May this sweet requited love drive away every sorrow; one heart, one soul—may they joyously keep for you that precious gift of God, as long as we are in this vale of tears!

### 68 · PHILIPP HEINRICH ERLEBACH (1657–1714),

*Kommt, ihr Stunden*

Hoff - nung-los Ganz ver - las - sen.

1.

Kommt, ihr Stunden, macht mich frei
Von des Lebens Tyrannei.
Glaubt, ich weiss mich nicht zu fassen,
Meine Qual ist allzu gross;
Ich steh aller Hoffnung-los ganz verlassen.
Kommt, ihr Stunden, macht mich frei . . .

Come, oh Time, free me from the tyranny of life.
Believe me, I cannot contain myself; my torment
is too great. I have lost all hope. Come, oh Time,
free me from the tyranny of life.

2.

Selbst die Freunde stellen sich,
Wenn ich klage, wider mich.
Sie verlachen mein Verderben,
Meine Pein mehrt ihren Scherz;
Will mein abgezehrtes Herz gleich ersterbe.
Selbst die Freunde . . . etc.

Even my friends turn against me when I mourn.
They laugh at my undoing; my suffering increases
their joking. My wasted heart will soon die. Even
my friends . . . etc.

3.

Was mein Leben sonst erfreut,
Bringt mir jetzo Traurigkeit,
Wo ich vormals Lust gefunden,
Fühl ich jetzt nur Weh und Ach,
Darum meiner Tränen Bach alle Stunden.
Was mein Leben . . . etc.

What I once enjoyed now brings me sadness.
When I once felt pleasure, now I feel only pain
and suffering. And so the stream of my tears flows
on eternally. What I once . . . etc.

4.

Hört der Himmel denn doch nicht,
Was mein Herze klagend spricht?
Klipp und Felsen, Flut und Wellen,
Drohen mir Gefahr und Not;
Ach mein schwankes Hoffnungsboot will zerschel-
len. Hört der Himmel . . . etc.

Does Heaven not hear what my sad heart speaks?
Crag and mountain, stream and fountain, bring
me only peril and distress. The frail boat of my
hope is being wrecked. Does Heaven . . . etc.

5.

Ach, ihr Stunden, macht mich los,
Mein Verhängnis ist zu gross.
Lasst mich bald das Ufer küssen,
Jammerwelt, dir sag ich auf.
Himmel, du wirst meinen Lauf glücklich schlies-
sen! Ach, ihr Stunden . . . etc.

Oh Time, free me, my fate is too dire. Oh world
of woes, I call upon you to let me kiss your shore
goodbye. Heaven, I will be glad when you bring
the course of my life to an end. Oh Time, free me
. . . etc.

## 69 · FRIEDRICH WILHELM ZACHOW (Zachau?) (1663–1712),

*Ruhe, Friede, Freud' und Wonne*

auf, ih - re Strahl - en dring - en___ vor: O wie wallt,___

O wie wallt___ mein Herz em - por; weg mit

Trau - ern, Furcht und Za - gen, da dies___ hel - -

-le Freu - den - licht, Got - tes Geist, in mei - ner___ See - le,

Durch die dunk - len Schat - ten bricht.

Ruhe, Friede, Freud' und Wonne
Gottes Geist, der Freuden Sonne,
gehn in meinem Herzen auf,
ihre Strahlen dringen vor:
O wie wallt mein Herz empor;
weg mit Trauern, Furcht und Zagen,
da dies helle Freuenlicht,
Gottes Geist in meiner Seele,
Durch die dunklen Schatten bricht.

Rest, Peace, Joy, and Rapture,
The spirit of God, the sun of Joy,
Flood my heart, their rays penetrate.
How my heart rises up!
Away with sadness, fear, and timidity,
For this clear rejoicing, the spirit of God,
Bursts through the dark shadows in my heart.

## 70 · JOHANN THEIL(E)  (1646–1724),

*Jesu, mein Herr und Gott*

- su, mein __Herr und __Gott al-lein, wie süss_ist_mir, wie süss_ist_mir der_Na - me __

dein, wie süss_ist_mir der_ Na - me dein. Es kann kein Traü -

- me sein so teuer, dein süs-ser Na - me er-freu - et viel mehr.

Kein E - lend mag so bit-ter sein, kein

E‑lend mag so bit‑ter sein, dein süs‑ser Trost er‑leuch‑tet _ fein.

Es kann, es kann — kein Traü‑me sein so teuer,

dein süs - ser Trost er leuch - tet fein.    Drum will ich weil ich le - be noch,

der Kreuz dich wil - lig tra - gen nach; Mein Gott, mach mich dar - zu be - reit,

und dien' zum bes - ten al - le Zeit.

Er-halt mein Herz im glau - ben rein, so leb' und sterb' ich dir___ al-lein.

Je - su, mein Trost, hör' mein ___ Be-gier, Ach, ___ mein Hei - land, wär' ich bei dir!

Jesu, mein Herr und Gott allein,
wie süss ist mir der Name dein.
Es kann kein Traüme sein so teuer,
dein süsser Name erfreuet viel mehr.
Kein Elend mag so bitter sein,
dein süsser Trost erleuchtet fein.
Drum will ich weil ich lebe noch,
der Kreuz dich willig tragen nach;
Mein Gott, mach mich darzu bereit,
und dien' zum besten alle Zeit.
Erhalt mein Herz im glauben rein,
so leb' und sterb' ich dir allein.
Jesu, mein Trost, hör mein Begier,
Ach, mein Heiland, wär ich bei dir!
Amen.

Jesus, my only Lord and God, how sweet is your name to me. No dream can be so delightful, that your sweet name does not give me greater pleasure. No pain can be so bitter that your sweet consolation does not ease it. So long as I live, I will bear the cross after you; my God, make me worthy of it and of serving you as best as I can, at all times. Keep my heart in pure faith, that I may live and die for you alone. Jesus, my comfort, hear my desire; my salvation, I would be with you. Amen.

### 71 · REINHARD KEISER (1674–1739),

*Per compiacerti, o cara* from *L'inganno fedele*

Per com-pia-cer - ti,o ca - ra! O ca - ra,__ ca - ra tut - to,     tut - to,

tut-to fa-rà il mio cor,        tut-to fa-rà il mio cor.

Per com-pia-cer - ti,o ca - ra! O ca - ra, ca - ra, ca - ra!     tut - to,        tut - to,

tut-to fa - rà il mio cor,        tut-to, tut-to, tut-to fa-rà il mio cor.

Fine

Gra -

Fine

-di - to, o non a - ma - to,    gra-di-to,    gra - di-to, o non _ a - ma - to,

**30**

scher-ni - to,    scher-ni - to, scher-ni-to, o - ver sprez-za  - - - -

- to,    a - do - re - rò co - stan - te tuo a-ma - bi - le _ ri - gor,    a -

Per compiacerti, o cara,
tutto farà il mio cor.
Gradito, o non amato,
schernito, over sprezzato,
adorerò costante tuo amabile rigor.

My heart will do anything to please you, my dear.
Loved or not loved, scorned or despised, I, faithful, will adore your lovable steadfastness.

## 72 · GEORGE FRIDERIC HANDEL (1685–1759),

*Il gelsomino* [Cantata No. 63]

Son gel - so - mi - no, son___ pic - ciol___

fio - re,   ma, più___ del___ gi - glio, son___ a - mo - ro - se,___

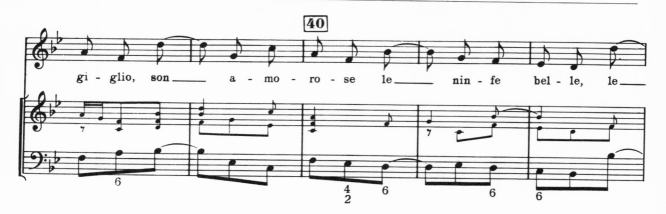

gi - glio, son___ a - mo - ro - se le___ nin - fe bel - le, le___

___ nin - fe bel - le del__ mio can - dor, del__ mio can - dor,

del__ mio__ can - dor, ma___ più del gi - glio son___ a - mo -

-ro - se le nin - fe bel - le,___ le nin - fe bel - le

del___ mio    can - dor.

*Fine*

*Fine*

Han  le  mie  fo - glie  sì___  gra - to  o - do - re    che  più  so -

-a - ve  non___  han  le  ro - se,___  ben - chè  re - gi - ne___

de - gli al - tri fior, han ____ le mie ____ fo - glie sì ____ gra - to o -

-do - re che ____ più ____ so - a - ve non ____ han le ____ ro - se, ben -

-chè ____ re - gi - ne de ____ gli al - tri fior, _____

*Da capo al Fine*

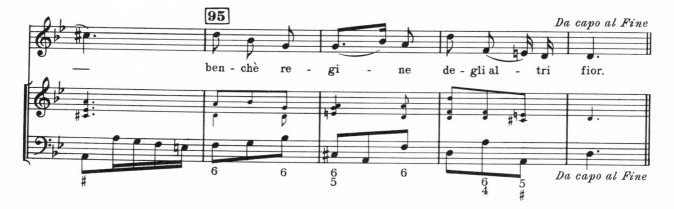

ben - chè re - gi - ne de - gli al - tri fior.

*Da capo al Fine*

**Recitativo**

Tre-mo-lan-te e leg-gie-ro stret-to fra ver-di   e   ben di-spo-ste fron-de,   bel ve-

-der-mi or-na-men-to a un va-go cri-ne;   e lie-ve-men-te   ver la guan-cia io stes-so   dar   e

pren-der bel-lez-za   a un tem-po i-stes-so.   Quand'u-no stuol di fior   me-co ab-bel-

-li-sce   u-na bril-lan-te   te-sta   o un mol-le   se-no,   fas-si di me più

sti-ma, e la can-di-da man di chi s'a-dor-na, mi pon'com'in tri-on-fo a gli al-tri in ci-ma.

Aria 2 [Larghetto ♩.= M.M. 58]

Spes-so mi sen - to dir da vez - zo-set - ta boc - ca: sei

bel - lo, gra-to e a-ma - bi-le, o ca-ro gel-so-min, ca-ro sei bel -

-lo,        sei gra - to,        sei bel - lo, gra - to e a - ma - bi - le,  o  ca - ro gel - so-

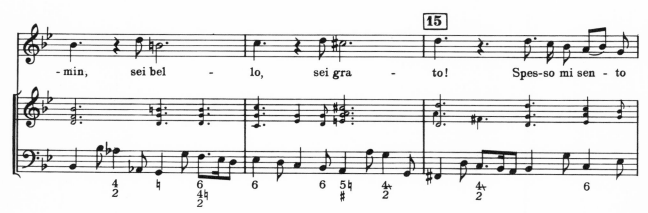

-min,        sei bel - lo,        sei gra - to!      Spes-so mi sen - to

dir        da vez - zo - set - ta boc - ca,        da vez - zo - set - ta

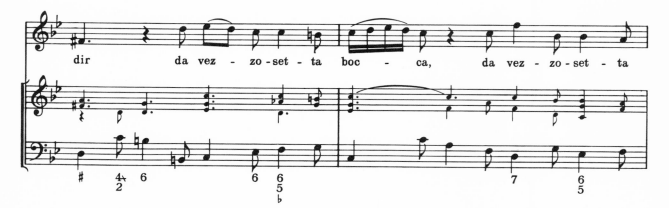

boc - ca:        sei bel - lo, gra - to e a - ma - bi - le,  o — ca - ro gel - so - min,  ca - ro        sei

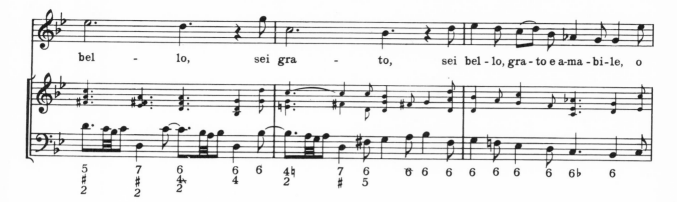

bel - lo, sei gra - to, sei bel - lo, gra - to e a - ma - bi - le, o

ca - ro gel - so - min, ca - ro, o ca - ro gel - so - min!

E spes-so in un so-spir, che

pas - sa e che mi toc - ca, go - do sen-tir che in-vi-dia-no gli a-man-ti il mio de-stin, e spes -

Aria 1

Son gelsomino, son picciol fiore,
ma, più del giglio, son amorose
le ninfe belle del mio candor.
Han le mie foglie sì grato odore
che più soave non han le rose,
benchè regine degli altri fior.

I am the jasmine, a little flower, but the fair
nymphs enjoy my whiteness more than that of the
lily. My petals have a perfume more sweet even
than the rose, though she is queen of the other
flowers.

Recitative

Tremolante e leggiero,
stretto fra verdi e ben disposte fronde,
bel vedermi ornamenta a un vago crine;
e lievemente ver la guancia io stesso
dar e prender bellezza a un tempo istesso.
Quand' uno stuol di fior meco abbellisce
una brillante testa o un molle seno,
fassi di me più stima,
e la candida man di chi s'adorna,
mi pon' com' in trionfo a gli altri in cima.

Trembling and light, my green leaves tightly ar-
ranged, it is good to see me ornamenting curly
locks and gaily giving beauty to a face and receiv-
ing beauty from it. Often, when a bouquet of flowers ornaments a shining head or a soft bosom, I
am the more highly esteemed, and the fair hand
of the woman who adorns herself places me at the
very top, in triumph over the others.

Aria 2

Spesso mi sento dir
da vezzosetta bocca:
sei bello, grato e amabile, o caro gelsomin!
che passa e che mi tocca,
godo sentir che invidiano
E spesso in un sospir,
gli amanti il mio destin.

I often hear a sweet mouth say, "You are beautiful, pleasing and lovely, oh dear jasmine!" And
often, in a passing sigh which touches me, I enjoy
hearing that lovers envy me my destiny.

73 · JOHANN SEBASTIAN BACH   (1685–1750),

Recitative, *Wir beten zu dem Tempel an*
and Aria, *Höchster, mache deine Güte* from
Cantata No. 51, *Jauchzet Gott in alle Landen* [BWV 51]

- len, so kann ein schlech-tes Lob ihm den-noch wohl-ge-fal-len.

Aria [♩. = M.M. 66]

Sop.

Höch - ster,

Höch-ster, ma - che dei - ne Gü te fer - ner al - le Mor - gen neu, al - le Mor-

- gen neu, al - le Mor - gen neu,_____ Höch-

hei - ssen.                                        Höch -       ster,

*Recitative*

Wir beten zu dem Tempel an, da Gottes Ehre wohnet, da dessen Treu', so täglich neu, mit lauter Segen lohnet. Wir preisen, Was Er an uns hat getan.
Muss gleich der schwache Mund von seinen Wundern lallen, so kann ein schlechtes Lob ihm dennoch wohlgefallen.

We worship in the temple, where God's majesty dwells, from whence each day He bestows the pure blessing of His grace. We praise the Lord for all that He has done. Even though my feeble tongue can only stammer of His wonders, God is pleased with simple praise.

*Aria*

Höchster, mache dein Güte ferner alle Morgen neu.
So soll für die Vatertreu'
auch ein dankbares Gemüte durch ein frommes Leben weisen,
dass wir deiner Kinder heissen.

Father most high, grant us Thy favor each new day. So, for Thy fatherly goodness, shall we show a thankful spirit through pious lives, so that we may be called Thy children.

## 74 · JOHANN ADOLPHE HASSE (1699–1783),

*Orgoglioso fiumicello* from the cantata *L'inciampo*

Or - go - glio - so———— fiu - mi - cel - lo,———— chi t'ac - creb - be i

* The figured bass was partially realized by the composer.

Or - go -

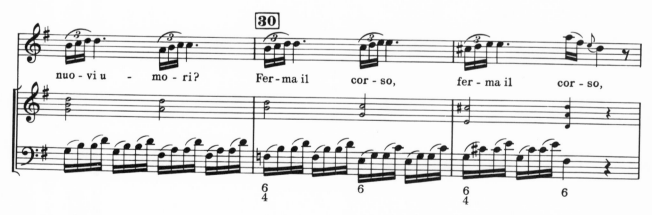

-glio - so ___ fiu - mi - cel - - - lo, chi t'ac - creb - be i

nuo - vi u - mo - ri? Fer - ma il cor - so, fer - ma il cor - so,

io va - do à Clo - ri; sco - pri il var - co, à Clo - - - - -

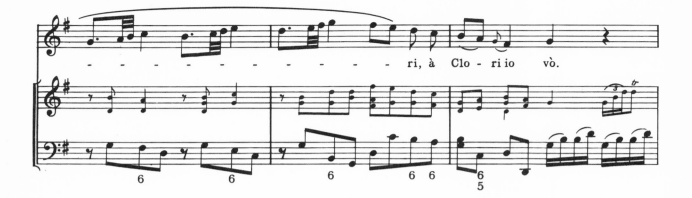

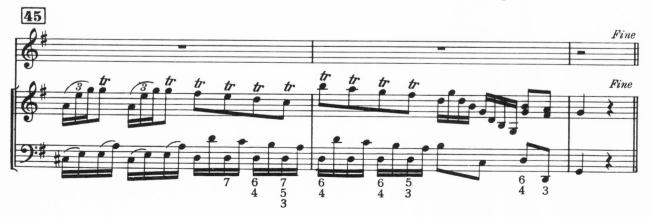

**Andante, ma poco**

Già m'at - ten-de al-l'al-tra spon - da: la - scia sol ch'io giun-ga à

le - i; po - scia in - on-da i cam - pi mie - i, nè di te mi la-gne -

-rò, nò, nè di

te mi la - gne - rò, di te, di

te,          non—mi la-gne - rò, nò,—— nò,—————— nò, non—mi la-gne - rò.

**[Recitativo]**

Ma      tu cre-sci fra tan-to.    Ec - co l'au-ro - ra;    Clo - ri m'at-ten-de,     ed

io m'ar-re-sto an-co - ra.          In - vi-do fiu-me!  E  quan-do  me-ri-tai  tan-to

sde-gno?  Io dal tuo let -to      al - lon-ta-nai gli ar-men-ti;          io sol col-te-si    a

t'e-du-cai gli al - lo - ri.    Al - lor  ba-gna-vi ap - pe - na  la più de-pres-sa a-

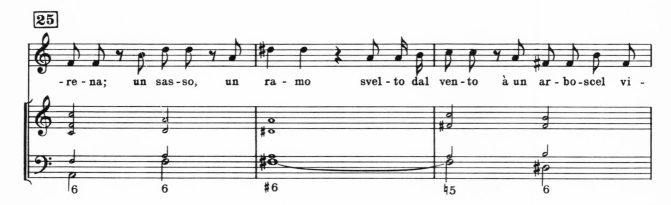

-re-na;  un sas-so,  un  ra - mo    svel-to dal ven-to  à un ar-bo-scel vi-

-ci - no    e - ra im-pac-cio ba-stan - te    al  tuo cam - mi - no.    Ed

or, can-gia-to in fiu-me,    gon-fio d'ac-que  e di spu-me,    stre-pi-to-so ri-vol-gi ar-bo-ri e

sas-si,      sde-gni le spon-de,      e non m'a - scol - ti,   e   pas-si.

**Allegretto**

Ri - tor - ne -

-rai___ fra po - co, po - ve - ro___ ru - scel - let - to,

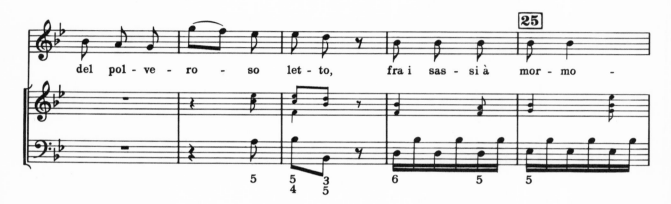

del pol - ve - ro - so let - to, fra i sas - si à mor - mo -

- rar,   à    mor - mo - rar         fra i    sas - si à

mor - mo - rar,___

à mor - mo -

-rar, à mor - mo - rar.

Ri - tor - ne - rai____ fra

po - co,     po - ve - ro____ ru - scel - let - to,     del pol - ve -

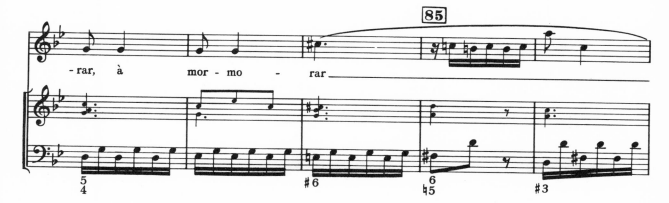

si, fra i sas - si à mor - mo -

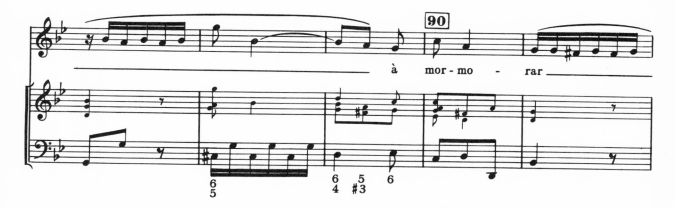

- rar, à mor - mo - rar _____

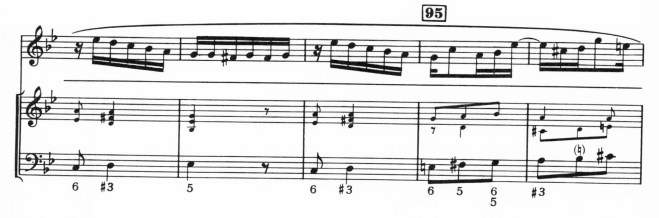

à mor - mo - rar _____

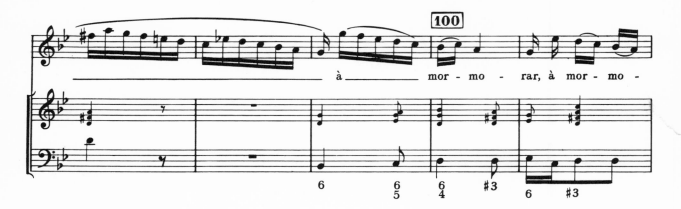

à _____ mor - mo - rar, à mor - mo -

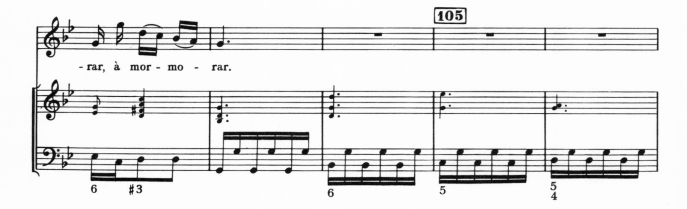

- rar, à mor - mo - rar.

*Fine*

*Fine*

Ti var - che - rò ____ per gio - co, di - stur - be - rò ____ quel -

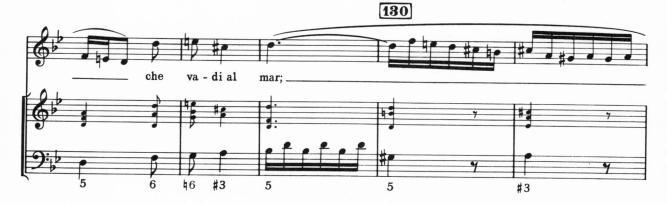

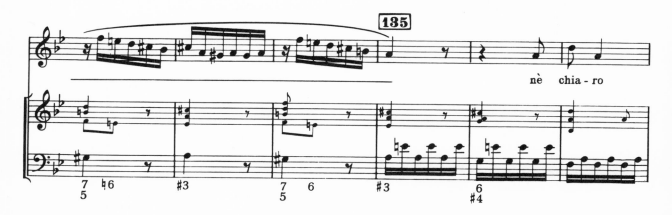

*Da capo al Fine*

fra    le    spon - de, __ fa - rò che _____ va - di al    mar.

*Da capo al Fine*

*Aria I*

Orgoglioso fiumicello, chi t'accrebbe i nuovi umori?
Ferma il corso, io vado à Clori.
Scopro il varco, à Clori io vò.
Già m'attende all' altra sponda:
Lascia sol ch'io giunga à lei; poscia inonda
I campi miei, nè di te me lagnerò.

Oh prideful stream, who is aggravating your ill will? Stop your flow. I am going to Chloris. Uncover the ford—I go to my Chloris! Already she is waiting for me on the other bank. Only let me reach her, then you can flood my fields and I won't complain to you.

*Recitative*

Ma tu cresci fra tanto. Ecco l'aurora;
Clori m'attende, ed io m'arresto ancora.
Invido fiume! e quando meritai
Tanto sdegno? Io dal tuo letto allontanai
Gli armenti; io sol coltesi a Nice ed a Licori
Del tuo margine i fiori;
E spesso, ingrato, per non scemarti umor, numi, il sapete,
Pochi stille ho negato alla mia sete.
Se ignoto altrui non sei,
Opra è de' versi miei.
Se passi ombroso infra gli estivi ardori,
In su le sponde io t'educai gli allori.
Allor bagnavi appena la più depressa arene;
Un sasso, un ramo svelto dal vento e un arboscel vicino
Era impaccio bastante al tuo cammino.
Ed or, cangiato in fiume,
Gonfio d'acque e di spume,
Strepitoso rivolgi arbori e sassi,
Sdegni le sponde, e non m'ascolti, e passi.

But you are getting bigger all the time! Now it is dawn. Chloris awaits me and I still remain here. Ungrateful river! When have I deserved such treatment? I freed your bed of debris; I picked the flowers from your banks for Nice and for Licori; and often, ungrateful that you are, in order not to deprive you of water, oh Divinity, I deprived my own thirst of a few drops. If you are not unknown to other people, it is the work of my verses. If you flow along in the shade during the heat of the summer, I cultivated the laurel bushes along your banks. Then you scarcely wet the sands of your bed; a stone, a branch blown by the wind from a nearby bush was an obstacle in your path. And now, grown to be a river, swollen with water and foam, you roll riotously along trees and boulders, you spurn your banks, you refuse to listen to me and go on your way.

*Aria II*

Ritornerai fra poco, povero ruscelletto,
Del polveroso letto,
Fra i sassi à mormorar.
Ti varcherò per gioco,
Disturberò quell'onde,
Nè chiaro fra le sponde,
Farò che vadi al mar.

You will soon return, poor little brook, to murmuring among the stones. I will cross over you just for play. I will muddy your waters, and I will see to it that you do not flow quite clear between your banks to the sea.

## 75 · JOHANNES SIGISMUND SCHOLZ (SPERONTES) (1705–1750),

*Ich bin nun wie ich bin*

Ich _ bin nun wie ich _ bin,    und bleib _ bei mei - ner _
an - de - re _ sich _

Mo -    de, wie Hans _ in _ sei - nem _    So -    de: Nennt
krän -    ken So spricht _ mein _ froh - es _    Den -    ken. Ihr

es auch ei - gen Sinn,    Ich bin nun wie ich bin.
Gril - len im - mer - hin!    Ich bin nun wie ich bin.

Schlecht, recht und doch __ ma - nier - lich, nicht __

kost - bar a - ber __ zier - lich, Das ist mein Sym - bo -

-lum, Was scher' ich __ mich __ da - rum! Wenn

*Dal ℅ al Fine*

**1.**

Ich bin nun wie ich bin,
und bleib bei meiner Mode,
wie Hans in seinem Sode:
Nennt es auch eigen Sinn, Ich bin nun wie ich
    bin.
Schlecht, recht und doch manierlich,
nicht kostbar aber zierlich,
Das ist mein Symbolum, Was scher' ich mich
    darum!
Wenn andere sich kränken
So spricht mein frohen Denken.
Ihr Grillen immerhin! Ich bin nun wie ich bin!

I am the way I am, and stick to my own fashion,
like Hans in his own way—call it my own true
nature—I am the way I am. Bad, good, and even
polished; not costly but decorative, that is what I
stand for. What do I care about anything else?

2.

Seht meinen Wandel an,
den ich alltäglich führe!
Hab' ich beim Wein und Biere was böses noch
  getan?
Seht meinen Wandel an!
Wenn ich zum öftern sitze
Der Arbeit Last und Hitze Erdulde, weil ich
  kann:
Was liegt als denn daran?
Wenn ich zur Lust und Freude,
Herz, Mund, und Augen weide,
Verstumme, falscher Wahn! Seht meinen Wandel
  an!

Look at the way I live all the time. Have I in my cups ever done anything bad? Just look at the way I live! If I often sit and avoid the labor and heat of work while I can, what is the matter with that? If I delight my heart, my mouth, and my eyes in pleasure and happiness, be still false rumor! Look at the way I live!

3.

Es ist mir einerlei!
Kein Mensch kann unter allen auch allen wohlge-
  fallen.
Dies ist mein trost dabei: es ist mir einerlei!
Will mich das Glücke hassen,
und alle Welt verlassen?
Mein gut' Gewissen lacht,
wenn Blitz und Donner kracht.
Man sieht mich nicht erheben,
viel minder nachzugeben,
Es sei es wie es sei, es ist mir einerlei.

It's all one to me! No man can give pleasure to everyone in every way. This is my comforting thought: it's all one to me! Will happiness pass me by and the whole world cast me out? My good conscience just laughs when lightning crashes and thunder roars. No one ever sees me exalt myself, even less debase myself. Let things be as they may be—it's all one to me!

4.

Dies ist mein fester Schluss!
Nichts soll mich auch bewegen, den Vorsatz abzu-
  legen,
Wenn ich auch sterben muss.
Dies ist mein fester Schluss!
Durch dicke, wie durch dünne,
lauf' ich mit frohen Sinne, und immer frohen
  Mut:
so gehet alles gut:
So kann ich mit Vergnügen
Welt, Gluck und Neid besiegen,
So macht mir nichts Verdruss; dies ist mein fester
  Schluss!

This is my firm conclusion: nothing can make me change, to put aside all planning, since I must die soon! This is my firm conclusion. Through thick and thin, I am with happy mind and disposition always gay. All goes well! Thus I can happily do without the World, Happiness, and Envy. Nothing makes me unhappy. This is my firm conclusion.

# Historical Notes

## 1 · ANONYMOUS,
### Occhi de l'alma mia

Neapolitan *villanellas*—light, sentimental songs, somewhat rustic in character—were extremely popular during the sixteenth century, and *Occhi de l'alma mia* was one of the best liked. The verses appear in at least four collections of poetry and were set polyphonically by several of the foremost composers of the day. This version for bass voice with lute accompaniment may possibly be the model on which the polyphonic settings were based; on the other hand, it may be a transcription of a polyphonic version.

Source: Lucca, Biblioteca Communale, MS 774, fol. 31, lute tablature; fol. 47, vocal part, written in the bass clef in mensural notation.

## 2,3 · COSIMO BOTTEGARI,
### Aria da cantar stanze and Morte da me

In the Estense Library at Modena there exists a fascinating human and musical document, a court musician's songbook, the work of Cosimo Bottegari (1554–1620). It is an anthology of songs and instrumental music, as well as an account book and personal journal. Bottegari was of noble Florentine birth and was married to a noble Florentine lady. He was for some time at the court of Bavaria, where he was one of the favorites of Duke Albert V. Returning to Florence, he entered the service of the Medici. At the court of Ferdinand he was a favorite lutenist and singer. Bottegari was no wandering minstrel but a real troubadour, a man of substance and marked musical talent which he used for the amusement and edification of his social circle and noble patrons.

*Arie senza parole* or *arie da cantar stanze* were an important part of any lutenist-singer's repertory in the 16th century. With such ready-made, all-purpose melodies, any poem of a certain stanzaic pattern could be sung or recited to music at a moment's notice, for it was customary to sing the praises of a patron or a beautiful lady to such tunes. This *aria da stanza* is for

any verse with 11-syllable lines, but not necessarily *ottave*. Bottegari's textual underlay and the directions "without repeating (the last phrase) return to the beginning" show the manner in which such *arie* were sung. Arias for ottavas, sonnets, and the three-line stanza called *terza rima* also existed. (See *Bottegari Lutebook*, Nos. 4, 62, 63.)

Although *Morte da me* is a lute song dating from well before 1590, it has all the earmarks of monody as practiced by Caccini and the monodists of the early years of the 17th century. The text is expressive and the accompaniment is a simple harmonic support. Bottegari was a member of the Medici *cappella* during the years that Peri and Caccini were there; he was therefore fully aware of the ideas of the Camerata regarding solo song and the pieces in his Lutebook strongly reflect the new tendencies. See *A Court Musician's Songbook: Modena MS C311*, in *Journal of the American Musicological Society*, IX (1956), 177–92.

Source: 2. Modena, Bibl. Estense, Ms.C311, fol. 21v. Modern edition: C. MacClintock, *The Bottegari Lutebook* (Wellesley edition no. 8, 1965.)
3. Modena, Bibl. Estense, MS. C311, fol. 22v. Modern edition as above.

## 4 · LEONORA ORSINA,
### Per pianto la mia carne

The music for this setting of Sannazaro's poem is attributed (or perhaps dedicated) to the "Illustrissima et Eccellentissima Signora Leonora Orsina, Duchessa di Segni." She and her husband were part of the brilliant court of Francesco de' Medici, Grand Duke of Tuscany, and his beautiful Venetian spouse Bianca Capello, during their reign 1574–1587. Leonora and many other ladies of the court were well-trained singers and, apparently, composers as well. This little piece appears to be one of the earliest solo songs with what normally would have been "improvised" ornaments written out. In the manuscript a small a,b,c in the vocal part indicates where the *fioritura* is to be inserted and the embellishments, with corresponding letters, are notated at the bottom of the page.

Source: Modena, Biblioteca Estense, MS C311, fol. 5v.
Lute tablature with vocal part in mensural notation.

### 5 · HIPPOLITO TROMBONCINO,
*Io son ferito*

The art of "diminution," or breaking up long note-values into smaller ones by means of rapid passages or ornaments of one kind or another, was practiced by virtuoso singers during the 16th and 17th centuries and greatly appreciated by their auditors. Hippolito Tromboncino (fl. 1575–1620) was one of a group of Venetian *virtuosi* famous for artistic performances. Little else is known about him, and the only extant examples of his songs are preserved in Bottegari's songbook. *Io son ferito* is one of the rare examples of a song with written-out diminutions and illustrates perfectly the rules for adding embellishments and making *passaggi* and *diminutioni* given by such writers as Bassano, Bovicelli, and Conforto in their instruction books.

Source: Modena, Biblioteca Estense, MS C311. fol. 29v–30.
Lute tablature with vocal part in mensural notation.

### 6 · JACOPO PERI,
*Tu dormi*

Jacopo Peri (1561–1633) was of noble Florentine origin and served the Medici family in that city in the capacities of singer, composer, and principal director of music and musicians. He was an accomplished performer and so immensely popular that he was known to his contemporaries as *Il Zazzarino* (the fair-haired boy) in reference to his long golden curls.

Peri became one of the most active members of that famous Florentine *Camerata* which conceived the idea of reviving the mode of recitation in music which they believed was characteristic of the Greeks. In pursuit of this idea Peri stands out with his music for the opera *Dafne*, now unfortunately surviving only in fragments; originally performed in 1597, it is therefore the first modern opera. A second work, *Euridice* (1600), has survived in its entirety.

Peri also played a very important role in the early chamber monody, his collection *Le varie musiche* (1609) containing several monodies in the true "camerata" style, in which the music is somewhat subordinated to the poetic and expressive line. The present *Tu dormi* exemplifies almost to perfection the ideas of the Camerata about monody; it is strophic (then the preferred form) with the bass as well as the vocal part

treated rather freely. This song is not contained in *Le varie musiche,* but exists in at least two MSS. The present version is the one copied and performed by the famous singer, Luigi Rossi, and differs from that in the Rudnice MS, published by R. Haas in *Die Musik des Barocks.*

Source: British Museum, Add. MSS 30, 419. fol. 42v–43v.

### 7,8 · GIULIO CACCINI,
*Sfogava con le stelle*
and *Ohimè, se tant' amate*

Giulio Caccini (1545–1618), known also as Giulio Romano, lived practically his whole life in Florence as vocal and instrumental musician in the service of the Medici court. He came there as a young man in 1563 and soon achieved great renown as "canto famoso," a brilliant soprano virtuoso. We can assume he was not a castrato, since he fathered several daughters who also became artists of repute. His voice may have been a very high tenor. He also soon won a fine reputation as composer. He tried his hand at opera as collaborator with Peri and later as his rival, but Caccini's chief claim to fame lies in his monodies and in the preface to his volume *Le nuove musiche,* published in 1602. Here he describes in some detail his technique and that of his contemporaries in the performance of vocal music. In addition to *Le nuove musiche* of 1602, which by the way, includes his immensely popular *Amarilli mia bella,* Caccini published *Fuggilotio musicale,* which means Musical Pastime in 1610, and in 1614 another, quite different *Nuove musiche.*

*Sfogava con le stelle* is from the first *Nuove musiche* and demonstrates the quasi-recitando style so much favored by the monodists as well as the use of vocal *accenti. Ohimè, se tant' amate,* which exemplifies Caccini's idea of "speaking, as it were, in harmony" is from his *Fuggilotio musicale.*

Sources: 7. *Le nuove musiche,* Florence, 1602, p. 13.
8. *Fuggilotio musicale,* 2nd ed., Venice, 1613, p. 6.

### 9,10 · FRANCESCO RASI,
*Indarno Febo* and *Ahi, fuggitivo ben*

Francesco Rasi (fl. 1590–1625), one of Caccini's pupils and a leading Florentine singer, was also an outstanding early monodist. He was noted for his expressive singing and for his taste in improvised embellishments. In his first published book of songs with *basso continuo* (1608), many of the ornaments as sung by Rasi himself are written out. Here are the *esclamazioni, tirate, passaggi,* of which Caccini spoke in his preface to *Le nuove musiche,* used with restraint to enhance the vocal line. In both of the arias chosen for this collection, the embellishments are Rasi's own. *Indarno Febo,* on a poem by Gabriello Chiabrera, is called a *madrigal.* It is worthy of note that Rasi was one of the first composers to acknowledge in print the poets who provided him with texts. *Ahi, fuggitivo ben* is an aria over a ground bass, the famous "Ruggiero", so popular during the first half of the 17th century. Here the bass melody is used four times, with a little codetta to close. The words are by Rasi himself.

Source: 9. *Le Vaghezze di Musica, per una voce sola, di Francesco Rasi, Gentilhuomo Aretino, Raccolte da Don Bassano Casola, Vice Mastro di Cappella del Serenissimo di Mantova . . .* Venetia, A. Gardano, 1608. pp. 2v.
10. As above, p. 8v.

## 11 · JOHANN HIERONYMO KAPSBERGER,
### *Interrotte speranze*

Johann Hieronymo Kapsberger (c. 1575–1661), called in Italy "Giovanni Geronimo tedesco della Teorba", was a German nobleman. He settled early in Italy, first at Venice, then at Rome, where he became one of the most prominent performers on instruments of the lute family as well as one of the most prolific composers of his time for voice and stringed instruments. In the service of the Barberini family, he was the colleague of Frescobaldi and of D. Mazzochi. His abundant vocal compositions, which resemble strongly those of his northern contemporaries Peri and Rasi, aided in the dissemination of the monodic style. Among his works were technical studies on the chitarrone, several books of madrigals and villanelle with basso continuo and lute, theorbo, and guitar accompaniments, as well as arias, dances, lute music, an opera, and various sacred works. The volume from which this selection is taken is called *arie passeggiate* because the songs have the vocal embellishments written out. It is highly instructive for the performer who wishes to execute this early music in the proper style. Kapsberger gives not only the bass line for accompaniment but the chitarrone tablature as well (the bass is identical for both.) Our realization is simply that of the tablature with a few notes added (in smaller print) to fill out the harmony.

Source: *Libro Primo di Arie Passeggiate a una Voce con L'Intavolatura del Chitarrone del Sig. Gio. Girolamo Kapsberger, Nobile Alemanno . . .* Roma, 1612. (Aria no. 2)

## 12 · CLAUDIO MONTEVERDI,
### *Interrotte speranze*

Since Claudio Monteverdi (1567–1643) is well known as one of the great masters of Western music, there is no need to recapitulate his biography here, other than to remind the reader that he was a prolific writer of secular music—madrigals, dramatic works, songs—and a smaller number of sacred compositions, which include his brilliant *Vespro della Beata Vergine.* Monteverdi culminated the long line of avant-garde composers which began with Willaert and Rore, and his works summarize the "new" music, the revolutionary tendencies which altered the musical climate of the first part of the 17th century. In this respect he may be compared to Beethoven, Wagner, and Debussy.

*Interrotte speranze,* a chamber duet for two tenors, is in the best monodic style.

Source: *Concerto. Settimo libro de madrigali a 1, 2, 3, 4, & 6 voci, con altri generi de canti.* Venice, 1619. p. 94.

## 13,14 · SIGISMONDO D'INDIA,
### *Mentre che 'l cor* and *O del cielo d'Amor*

Sigismondo d'India (ca. 1582–?) was the scion of a noble Sicilian family. Little is known of his early life. In 1608 he was in Florence, where his music was sung by such famous singers as Caccini and Vittoria Archilei. From 1611 to 1623 he occupied the post of *maestro della musica di camera* at the court of Carlo Emmanuele I, Duke of Savoy, at Turin. From 1624 until his death he lived and worked in Rome, composing madrigals for five voices, vocal duets, four books of monodies, pastoral plays, ballets and other works for the stage. He seems to have been famous as a singer; in 1618 one of his editors declared him to have "no equal in solo song." From his varied production we present *Mentre che 'l cor* in purest monodic style and *O del cielo d'Amor,* an aria which is really a miniature *recitativo ed aria.*

Sources: 13. *Le musiche del Cavalier Sigismondo d'India, a una e due voci. Da Cantarsi nel Chitarrone, Clavicembalo, Arpa doppia, & altri stromenti da Corpo. Con alcune arie, con l'alfabeto per la Chitarra alla Spagnola. Libro Quarto . . .* In Venetia, appresso Alessandro Vincenti. 1621.
14. *Le Musiche del Cavalier Sigismondo d'India, Gentilhuomo del Serenissimo Prencipe Mauritio, Cardinale di Savoia. Da Cantarsi nel Chitarrone, Clavicembalo, Arpa doppia, & altri stromenti da Corpo. Libro Quinto . . .* In Venetia appresso Alessandro Vincenti. 1623.

## 15 · STEFANO LANDI,
### *Superbi colli*

Stefano Landi (ca. 1590–1655) was a Roman contralto and composer of at least two operas (the only one known today is *San Alessio,* 1632), numerous choral works, and five books of arias for one and two voices. The aria, *Superbi colli*, based on a favorite madrigal text by B. Castiglione, is for solo voice and basso continuo (possibly lute, theorbo, viol, or cembalo.) It is composed in two *partes*, like the older polyphonic madrigal, but the first part is in the new *stilo recitativo* and the second part in virtuoso vocal style. Thus, although not so indicated, it corresponds to the later *recitativo ed aria*. The brilliant singing and the wide range required of the bass voice was not unusual; there were a number of famous basses noted for their exceptional vocal range: Alessandro Merlo, Giovan Andrea napoletano, Melchior basso. May we point out the static quality of the accompaniment, so similar in style to Peri's.

Source: *Arie a una voce di Stefano Landi*. Venetia, Magni, 1620.

### 16,17 · CLAUDIO SARACENI,
### *De te parto* and *Mori, mi dice*

Claudio Saraceni or Saracini (1586–ca. 1649), "noble Senese," was an amateur composer who had studied briefly with Monteverdi, whom he admired greatly. He was one of the most advanced of the Italian monodists and his somewhat unorthodox harmonic progressions, frequent dissonant clashes, formidable leaps and augmented intervals place him in the same relation to the professional monodists as Gesualdo was to the madrigalists, his contemporaries. Whatever his shortcomings, Saraceni's settings of passionate, emotional texts are always sensitive and usually highly appropriate. His free, declamatory style is evident in the aria, *Da te parto*, dedicated to his father, Cavaliere Gherardo Saracini. The final phrase is a fine example of the vocal "trillo" as used by Caccini. In Saraceni's later books his style is less extreme. The second piece, although still displaying the heightened recitative style, is more melodious and graceful than the first, and somewhat sentimental.

Sources: 16. *Le Seconde Musiche di Claudio Saracini (detto Il Palusi) Nobile Senese. Per Cantar & Sonar nel Chitarrone, Arpicordo & altri Stromenti* . . . In Venetia, Appresso Alessandro Vincenti, 1620. p. 7.
17. *Le Quinte Musiche da Cantar e Sonar nel Chitarrone, Arpicordo, Arpa Doppia, & simili Instromenti. Di Claudio Saraceni, nobile senese* . . . Stampa del Gardano in Venetia. 1624, p. 5.

### 18 · ALESSANDRO GRANDI,
### *O quam tu pulchra es*

Alessandro Grandi (b. ?–1630) is associated mainly with Venice and the cathedral of St. Mark as singer and composer. He may have been a pupil of Giovanni Gabrieli. He was greatly esteemed by his contemporaries and was one of the outstanding composers of continuo madrigals and motets. His musical production was extensive, but little of it has survived; that little, however, shows him to have been one of the truly gifted composers of the day. He is known as the first composer to use the term *cantade*, by which he meant a strophic song with several verses sung to the same bass, not the sectional form with succession or alternation of *recitativo*, *arioso* and *aria* which the word connotes today. The motet, *O quam tu pulchra es*, actually has the structure of a cantata and is notable for its intense emotional quality as well as its firm organization by means of repeated thematic material.

Source: Leonardo Simonetti, *Ghirlanda sacra scielta da diversi eccellenti compositori de varij motetti a voce sola* . . . Venezia, Gardano, 1625, p. 32.

### 19 · GIACOMO CARISSIMI,
### *Nò, nò, mio core*

The life of Giacomo Carissimi (1605–1674) cannot rightly be described as adventurous or exciting. After various ecclesiastical posts at Tivoli and Assisi, he was appointed *Maestro di cappella* and organist at Sant' Apollinare in Rome and spent 45 years at that post until his death. Among his pupils were Bononcini, Cesti, and Alessandro Scarlatti.

Carissimi was one of the first to write long oratorios on sacred subjects. In his mind, these were to take the place of operas on similar themes, since oratorios did not demand presentation in a theatre but could be performed in church or even in a salon. Carissimi also wrote chamber cantatas, when they were at the beginning of their development and their century-long popularity. He was a master of declamation, but there is also a substantial lyrical element in his writing for the solo voice. He "demonstrated that it is possible to give shape and direction to long compositions for solo voice without the assistance of stage action, by methods entirely in keeping with the character of the word" (*Grove's*, 5th ed., Vol. II, p. 71). His influence upon his contemporaries was profound.

*Nò, nò, mio core* exhibits both his lyrical gift and his qualities of craftsmanship in its balanced rondo-strophic structure. In Carissimi's own time this work was evidently widely circulated, for it exists in six different manuscripts. The version given here is from Br. Mus. Harley 1501, noted down in 1681 by Pietro Reggio, the Italian singer and lutenist. It is the same as that found in Br. Mus. Harley 1270, except that in our manuscript the refrain after strophes 2 and 3 is omitted.

Source: London, British Museum, MS Harley 1501, fols. 40v–42v.

## 20 · PIETRO FRANCESCO CAVALLI,
### *Tremulo spirito*

Son of a musician, Pietro Francesco Cavalli (1602–1676) became a singer himself at San Marco in Venice under Monteverdi, but soon began to write works for the theatre. During his long life he composed at least forty-two operas, or properly, *dramme per musica*. Immensely popular in Venice, his fame spread beyond the borders of Italy and he was called to Paris in 1660 for the marriage of Louis XIV, for which occasion he produced his opera *Xerse* in the grand gallery of the Louvre. He came to Paris once again in 1662, and at Innsbruck the same year he provided the music for the Austrian court's reception of Queen Christina.

In the early years of Venetian opera, spectacles and scenes of the supernatural combined with a taste for arias of highly emotional, affective nature. The *lamento* aria was one of the most popular and was usually written on a falling chromatic ground bass. This aria, *Tremulo spirito*, from Cavalli's *Didone* of 1641, one of the earliest of a type that persisted well into the eighteenth century, has a chromatic ground bass repeated four times. (We may note the similarity of the bass with that of a more famous example: Dido's Lament from Purcell's *Dido and Aeneas*.) A later and more elaborate example of the *lamento aria* may be seen in No. 23 by Barbara Strozzi.

Source: Venice, Biblioteca Marciana Cod. Contarini, Cavalli-Busenello *Didone* (1641) Act I, sc. 7.

## 21 · PIETRO ANTONIO CESTI,
### *Bella Clori*

Pietro Antonio Cesti (1623–1669) was one of the most popular and important Italian composers of the 17th century. He had a very checkered career; joining the Minorite friars in 1637 and calling himself Frate Antonio, he led a life that was anything but religious and was well-known for its irregularity. As a composer his main output consisted of seventeen operas in the Venetian style which received many performances and made him famous as a "miracolo della musica" throughout Europe.

But he did not confine himself to writing for the stage; his religious cantatas are masterpieces of the expressive style in which the music is eminently suited to the text. The same can be justly said of his profane compositions for the voice, both solo cantatas and concerted works. The Christ Church manuscript from which this cantata is taken contains eighteen secular and three religious cantatas, including his most famous work *Filiae Jerusalem*.

Source: Christ Church Library, Oxford. MS 83, pp. 1–6. (Of the four sections which comprise this cantata, only the first and fourth are here given.)

## 22 · LUIGI ROSSI,
### *La Gelosia*

Luigi Rossi (ca. 1598–1653) was singer, organist and composer. Born near Naples, he received his musical training there but early in his career moved to Rome, where he was successively in the service of the Borghese and the Barbarini families, as well as organist in various Roman churches. His cantata on the death of Gustavus Adolphus made him famous all over Europe. When the Barbarini fled to France under the persecution of Pope Innocent X, Rossi followed them, and his opera *Orfeo* was produced in Paris at the command of Cardinal Mazarin. It was a great artistic success, but was the object of violent attacks, really directed at Mazarin, on economic, political, and religious grounds. *Orfeo* was the first Italian opera produced in the French capital.

Though he wrote two operas, Rossi was chiefly known for his cantatas, of which he wrote more than a hundred. This form, perhaps better suited to his genius which was lyrical rather than dramatic, was in Rossi's hands sectional, with recitative and aria divisions, but somewhat free structurally. It does not adhere to the strict formal patterns of the later 17th-century cantata. His cantata *Gelosia*, on a text by Domenico Benigni, enjoyed wide renown in his day. It is found in six 17th-century manuscripts and was printed in *Ariette di musica* (Bracciano, Fei) in 1646. In more recent times it first became known through F. A. Gevaert's transcription (from MS. XY 8286 and F 664 in the library of the Brussels Conservatoire), published in *Gloires d'Italie* (1868).

Sources: *Les Gloires d'Italie* (Paris, 1868), p. 38.
   (Bass realized by the present editor)

## 23 · BARBARA STROZZI,
### *Lagrime mie*

Very little is known about the life of Barbara Strozzi (1620–?) except that she was the adopted daughter of Giulio Strozzi, famous poet and librettist for Monteverdi. We do know that she was a very accomplished singer, particularly popular in Venice at about the middle of the 17th century. Her four published volumes show her to have had exceptional talent as a composer, one who wrote in a highly individual, expressive vein.

Source: *Diporte di Euterpe ovvero Cantate & ariette a voce sola di Barbara Strozzi*, Opera settima . . . Venice, Alessandro Magni. 1659. p. 76ff.

## 24 · ALESSANDRO STRADELLA,
### *S'Amor m'annoda il piede*

The accounts of the life of Alessandro Stradella (1642–1682) are a curious mixture of fact and fiction.

He is known to have lived and taught in Venice, in Rome and in Turin; from the historical point of view he was chiefly associated with Rome and identified mainly with the musical life of that city. When he was in Venice he fell in love with a lady of noble birth affianced to an important functionary of the city. The two young people eloped, so enraging the jilted suitor that he engaged *bravi* to do away with Stradella. The young pair fled to Rome and later to Turin, where the assassins caught up with them and murdered the composer. This story is the basis of Flotow's opera *Alessandro Stradella*. Until recently most of Stradella's works have remained in manuscript, but an upsurge of interest in him is now bringing about their publication. He wrote sacred and secular music for both voice and instruments, several operas, motets, serenatas (Handel took an aria from one of these), oratorios, madrigals and cantatas. His oratorio, *San Giovanni Battista* (1676), is perhaps his greatest work. The short cantata *S'Amor m'annoda il piede* exemplifies his graceful, elegant style; in form it is not typical, for most of his cantatas are longer, with definite *recitativo*, *arioso* and *aria* sections.

Source: Cambridge, Fitzwilliam Museum MS 32 E 11, fol. 13. (It is found also in two other MSS: Paris, Bib. Nationale, Vsm IV-463; Rome, Vatican, Chigi Q IV 18.)

## 25 · ALESSANDRO SCARLATTI,
### Goderei sempre, crudele

Alessandro Scarlatti (1660–1725) was one of the great masters of Western music; his career and his compositions are so well-known that there is no need to recapitulate them here. As Professor Dent writes in his article in *Grove's Dictionary*, "He is the most important of that group of composers who succeeded the first pioneers of the monodic style, based upon the modern tonal system, and who moulded and developed a musical idiom which served as the language of musical expression down to the days of Beethoven." (5th ed., Vol. VII, p. 449.)

Scarlatti's production was tremendous. He is remembered nowadays mainly for his operas, of which he wrote some 125, but he also composed 150 oratorios, much instrumental music, church music, and, according to his own count, 600 cantatas for solo voice and continuo. By some critics he is described as the last great master of this form, which received its highest development at his hands.

The selections printed here are from a cantata dated 1695—the opening aria, next-to-last recitative and aria, and final aria. The three arias display his skill in using a motive consistently in the bass as well as his employment of the "motto" or *Devise* in the

first aria. This term is used to designate a type of aria in which the first few words and notes of the theme are sung by the voice alone, then, after a brief rest during which the continuo takes up the theme, the voice re-enters to sing the whole line or melody. It is really in the nature of a deceptive or false start which announces the theme alone.

Source: London, British Museum, MS Add. 14,164. fols. 1–2, 4–7ᵛ.

## 26 · BENEDETTO MARCELLO,
### Dal tribunal augusto

Benedetto Marcello (1686–1739) was a man of extraordinary and varied talents. A Venetian patrician, he became a prominent lawyer and administrator in his native city, being at one time a member of the famous Council of Forty, and administrative officer in various towns of the Republic. He was a poet of no mean ability, having written his own opera libretti and words for various other of his musical compositions. His satire on the theatre of his time, *Il Teatro alla moda*, was frequently reprinted and is most witty and amusing. He was also a musical theorist of distinction, a *Teoria musicale* being his chief contribution to the subject.

Marcello's fame, however, is firmly based on his music. He composed operas, pastorals, oratorios, *canzoni madrigaleschi*, and instrumental pieces. His greatest work, called one of the finest productions of musical literature, was his eight volume *Estro poetico-armonico, parafrasi sopra i primi 50 Psalmi, poesia di Girolamo Giustiniani* (Venice, 1724–26). The selection here printed is from this work.

Source: *Estro poetico-armonico* (Venice, 1724) Psalm 42 (1st verse only.) [43, King James version] (Taken from Hawkins' *History of Music*, XIX: CLXXX, p. 845)

## 27 · ANONYMOUS,
### The Willow Song

Many 16th and 17th century songs have the burden "O willow, willow, willow" or "Sing all a green willow." The most famous of them all is the one sung by Desdemona in Act IV, scene 3 of Shakespeare's *Othello*. Words similar to those given by Shakespeare are found in a lute song which exists in a manuscript volume dating from the early years of the 17th century. It is entirely possible that this tune is the one sung in the play. The words printed here are those given in the manuscript from which our transcription is taken.

Source: British Museum, MS Add. 15, 117.

## 28 · THOMAS MORLEY,
### *Come, Sorrow, come*

Thomas Morley (ca. 1557–1603), English composer, theorist, organist, was a pupil of William Byrd and one of the foremost musicians of his time: "he who did shine as the Sun in the Firmament of our Art," as Ravenscroft said after Morley's death. Although he wrote in almost all the forms of music then currently in use, Morley is remembered today chiefly for his *balletts*, light-hearted choral pieces modelled on those of G. G. Gastoldi, and for his important theoretical work, *A Plaine and Easie Introduction to Practicall Musicke,* 1597. About 1600 and for some time thereafter, songs "to sing and play to the Lute, with the Base Viole" were written by many composers. These are nothing more than songs with lute accompaniment and a viola da gamba doubling the lowest line in the manner of a *basso seguente.* Such songs may be considered transitions from the air with accompaniment fully written out to that with basso continuo alone. Morley's *Come, Sorrow, come* is one such. This piece, from his final work, shows a darker, more serious aspect of his music than do his earlier canzonets and madrigals with their lilting, dancing rhythms. The numerous false relations are characteristic of the English school at this period.

Source: *The First Booke of Ayres. Or Little Short Songs, to Sing and Play to the Lute, with the Base Viole. Newly Published by Thomas Morley, Bachiler of Musicke, and one of the Gent. of her Maiesties Royal Chappel.* Imprinted at London . . . 1600. (No. 12)

## 29 · PHILIP ROSSETER,
### *And would you see my mistress' face*

Philip Rosseter (c. 1575–1623) was a lutenist in the court of James I. He was closely associated with Thomas Campian, twenty-one of whose songs (on his own poems) appeared in the first part of Rosseter's *Book of Ayres.* It is thought by some that Campian provided the words for Rosseter's songs, but there is no evidence for this. Rosseter, like Campian, wrote lute songs of a simple, straightforward type for voice and lute. He did not make optional settings of his pieces for several voices, as did a number of the English lutenist composers. Rosseter's songs are graceful, singable, among the best of English lute song. This little strophic song is a fine example of the unaffected "ayre"—tonal, homophonic, with a tuneful, easily remembered melody.

Source: *A Booke of Ayres, set foorth to be song to the Lute, Orpherian and Base Violl, by Philip Rosseter Lutenist: And are to be solde at his house in Fleetestreete neer to the Grayhound.* At Lonond(*sic*) Printed by Peter Short, by

the assent of Thomas Morley. 1601. (No. 2, lute tablature.)

## 30,31 · JOHN DOWLAND,
### *If that a sinner's sighs* and *Lady, if you so spite me*

John Dowland (1563–1620) was an English (or Irish) lutenist, a virtuoso performer without rival in Europe and a highly skilled singer as well. His songs rank among the finest of all time and are as fresh today as when they were written. He published three books of *Songs or Ayres* and a fourth volume entitled *A Pilgrimes Solace;* three additional songs were printed by his son Robert in *A Musicall Banquet,* bringing the total to 87 songs in all. Most of his lute songs have alternative arrangements for four voices, and a few call for a treble and bass viol in addition to the lute. He was especially famed for his exquisite settings of sorrowful texts and his *Lachrymae, or Seven Teares, figured in seven passionate Pavans* for instruments was known throughout Europe.

*If that a sinner's sighs* is from the final set of songs, *A Pilgrimes Solace,* and shows Dowland's genius at its most mature. The grace and elegance of both vocal line and lute part, far removed from the square phrases of earlier lute songs, are characteristic of true through-composed solo song. *Lady, if you so spite me,* from *A Musicall Banquet,* shows Dowland's treatment of verse in a lighter vein.

Sources: 30. *A Pilgrimes Solace. Wherein is contained Musicall Harmonie of 3. 4. and 5. parts, to be sung and plaid with the Lute and Viols . . .* 1612.
31. *A Musicall Banquet: Furnished with varietie of delicious Ayres, collected out of the best Authors in English, French, Spanish and Italian . . .* 1610.

## 32,33 · WILLIAM CORKINE,
### *Each lovely grace* and *Beauty sat bathing*

William Corkine (fl. early 17th century), composer and lutenist, was probably also a player of the Lyra Viol, the viol that was strung and tuned like a lute and played from tablature. Almost nothing is known about him and his only extant works are two books of *Ayres* to be sung with the lute and/or bass viol. Singing to the bass viol alone was a practice current for some years, especially during the Commonwealth. *Each lovely grace* is an example of this practice; the accompaniment would have been only the bass line, with possibly a few chords provided by the viol player according to his taste and ability. Corkine's music is typical of the kind popular during the first quarter of the

17th century—rather naive, tuneful songs of not too great difficulty, suitable for the amateur. The pages of his books are printed with the parts facing, thus:

so that the performers could sit around a table. The words of the second song, by Anthony Munday, enjoyed some popularity, being also used by Pilkington for a lute song. Like Morley's *Little Short Ayres,* Corkine's song has both lute part and viol part to reinforce the lute, not as an optional accompaniment. The viol merely doubles the lute's bass line.

Sources: 32. *The Second Book of Ayres, some to sing and play to the Base Violl alone, others to be sung to the Lute and Base Violl, with new Corantoes, Pavins, Almaines, as also divers new Descants upon old Grounds set to the Lyra Violl.* London, 1612. (No. 1)

   33. *Ayres to Sing and play to the Lute and Basse Violl, with Pavins, Galliards, Almains and Corantoes for the Lyra Violl . . .* London, 1610. (No. 9; voice and lute tablature)

## 34 · ROBERT JOHNSON,
### *Care-charming sleep*

Robert Johnson (?–1633), English lutenist and composer, served as one of the king's musicians from 1604 on; his name appears in a list of Prince Henry's chapel in 1611 and he continued on under Charles I. He wrote for instruments as well as for voices and many of his compositions appeared in various anthologies of the time. He was highly esteemed for the songs he wrote for various masques and theatrical productions and was for some years associated with Beaumont and Fletcher, producing works for a number of their plays. The song here printed, from *Valentinian* (ca. 1619), occurs in Act V, scene 2, sung by an attendant before the dying Emperor and his wife. The embellishments given are those written in the manuscript, showing clearly the manner in which such songs were performed. This same song appears in other sources unadorned.

Source: British Museum, MS 11,608, fol. 36.

## 35 · GEORGE JEFFRIES,
### *Praise the Lord, O my soul*

George Jeffries (?–1685) was a composer of considerable prominence in the group of older contemporaries of Henry Purcell. Today, little is known about him except that during the 1640s he was at Oxford as organist in the chapel of Charles I, together with John Wilson. He was a prolific composer, mainly of sacred works (inasmuch as secular music was somewhat frowned upon during the Commonwealth), although a large number of his secular compositions for a variety of media also remain. Almost all of his work exists only in manuscript. The solo motet printed here must date from about 1660–62, a conjecture based on the fact that several pieces in the same manuscript from which these are taken are dated 1660–61. The text is from Psalm 104.

Source: British Museum, MS 10,338 (Jeffries' own autograph), fol. 104.

## 36,37 · HENRY LAWES,
### *Swift through the yielding air* and *Go, lovely Rose*

The Lawes brothers, Henry and William, were both members of the Royal Chapel under Charles I of England; both were performers, Henry a singer, William a lutenist; both were extremely successful and prolific composers. By a lucky chance, much of their music has been preserved.

Henry (1596–1662) was especially appreciated by the poets whose verse he used for his songs, largely because of his emphasis on the importance of the text. He began his composition with the words, to which he fitted a melody and then adjusted a bass. The list of poets who provided texts for him included Donne, Fletcher, Herrick, Lovelace, Jonson, and Milton, among others. He has been criticized for lacking melody, but his *aria parlante* style of composotion is calculated primarily to bring out the expression of the words rather than to provide a pleasing melody. He wrote both sacred and profane compositions and was called upon to provide the music for the famous performance of Milton's *Comus* at Ludlow Castle in 1634. (He took the part of the Attendant Spirit on that occasion.) He composed music for many of the court festivities and wrote several books of *Ayres and Dialogues* for one, two and three voices (1653, 1655, and 1658). At the Restoration, Lawes was given back many of the honors and positions at court which he had lost under Cromwell. He provided part of the music for the coronation ceremony of Charles II.

Source: *Select Ayres and Dialogues to sing to the Theorbo-Lute or Basse-Viol. Composed by Mr. Henry Lawes . . . And other Excellent Masters . . . The Second Book . . .* London, 1669, pp. 24, 43.

**38,39 · WILLIAM LAWES,**

*Had you but heard her sing!*
and *Gather your rose buds*

William Lawes (1602–1645) was just as much esteemed during his lifetime as his older brother Henry, and is judged a better, or at least more interesting composer, by posterity. He too was "musician in ordinary" to King Charles and was specially patronized by the Duke of Hertford. He wrote the music for Shirley's masque *The Triumph of Peace* in 1633, and Davenant's *The Triumph of the Prince d'amour* in 1635.

The younger Lawes's works comprise several books of songs, including the famous solo or part song *Gather ye rose buds,* and much instrumental music, mainly for a consort of viols. According to Groves' Dictionary "his scoring for musical combinations of chamber instruments is strikingly successful and his music for various forms of 'broken consorts' of the greatest interest."

Sources: British Museum, Add. MS 31,432 fol. 24.
*Ayres and Dialogues to sing to the Theorbo-Lute or Basse-Viol. Composed by Mr. Henry Lawes . . . And other Excellent Masters . . .* (Book I) . . . London, 1669, p. 101.

**40,41 · NICHOLAS LANIER(E) II**

*The Marigold* and *Love's Constancy*

Nicolas Lanier(e), (1588–1666), second of that name, was the most eminent member of a prominent musical family which flourished in England at the end of the 16th and beginning of the 17th centuries. All were associated with the English court, usually as wind instrument players. Nicholas II had many talents; he was a composer, singer, lutenist, painter of distinction, and evidently also a most accomplished courtier. As court musician for King Charles I, he composed music for several of the masques popular at the great festivities of the time. In 1617, his music for Ben Jonson's *Lovers made Men* is said to have introduced the *stylo recitativo* into England, and the work has been called "the first English lyric opera." For this performance Lanier not only composed the music and sang it, but also painted the scenery. Unfortunately the music is lost, as is most of his work.

He also composed music for Ben Jonson's *Masque of Anger* (1622) and other similar works. A cantata of his, a monodic dialogue, *Hero and Leander,* is the best basis for the statement that Lanier introduced Italian baroque vocal performance practice into England. A favorite of Charles I, he was made Master of the King's Music and was also sent to Italy by that monarch to buy paintings for the royal collection. At the Cromwellian revolution Lanier lost his positions and "was plundered not only of his fortune but of all his musical papers," accounting for the fact that relatively little of his abundant production has survived. After the Restoration in 1660, all of his honors were returned to him and he was once again a favorite at court; but he was now old, in poor health, and did not long survive to enjoy his prosperity.

From Lanier's few existing works it is clear that the high esteem in which he was held was merited. The songs here given have great charm and individual melodic turns that bespeak an unusual talent. Both *The Marigold* and *Love's Constancy* may be found not only in Playford's *Select Ayres* but in manuscript as well (Br. M. Add. MS 11608). In the latter the text of *The Marigold* is said to be "By His Majesty" (Charles I), and *Love's Constancy* has written-in ornamentation and differs somewhat from Playford's version.

Source: John Playford: *Select Ayres and Dialogues to Sing to the Theorbo-Lute or Basse-Viol, Composed by Mr. Henry Lawes . . . and other Excellent Masters.* The Second Book . . . London, 1669. (p. 54) also British Museum, Add. MS 11, 608, p. 59; British Museum, Add. MS 11, 608, fol. 61.

**42,43 · JOHN BLOW,**

*The Self-Banished* and
*Loving above Himself*

Although his reputation has faded considerably, partly under the attack of Dr. Burney, John Blow (1649–1708) was most highly esteemed by his contemporaries during the latter half of the 17th century. He was associated with the Courts of Charles II and James I in various important official capacities. The bulk of his music was ecclesiastical and ceremonial, sharing in the short-comings of such compositions by being for the most part conventional and dull.

But Blow had his moments and his share of genius, so some of his songs had an enduring popularity: "Thou flask once filled with glorious red", for one and "The Self-Banished" for another. No history of English song can leave Blow out. His miniature opera *Venus and Adonis,* probably written for Charles II, is, according to *Grove's Dictionary,* "the earliest extant example of genuine opera in English," being entirely English, and owing nothing to the Italians. Blow's songs for one, two, and three voices are contained in several collections, of which *Amphion Anglicus* (1700) is the most important. Both songs here presented are from that work.

Source: *Amphion Anglicus. A work of many compositions, for One, Two, Three and Four Voices: With several Accompagnements of Instrumental Musick, and a Thorow-Bass to each song: figur'd for an Organ, Harpsichord, or Theor-*

boe-Lute . . . By Dr. John Blow. . . . London
. . . 1700, p. 91; p. 20.

## 44,45,46 · HENRY PURCELL,

*Music for awhile* [Z. 583(2)],
*Winter's Song* [Z. 629(32b)],
and *Sweeter than Roses* [Z. 585(I)]

Henry Purcell (1659–1695) has always, from his own
time to the present, been hailed as one of the great
English composers. His biography is familiar and a
sizeable portion of his extensive production is well-
known. One of the qualities that contributes to Purcell's greatness is his remarkable ability to write for
the voice. A singer himself, Purcell's vocal music always shows a sure sense of vocal technique and of
what will be grateful and effective to the performer.
The anthems, odes, incidental songs for stage works,
the opera *Dido and Aeneas*, all exemplify his eloquent, expressive style. Certain songs have long enjoyed popularity due to their tunefulness and
sprightliness—*Man is for the Woman made, Nymphs
and Shepherds, I'll sail upon the dogstar*—and yet his
songs are still too little known. Among his great ones
are those on a ground bass and those of a descriptive,
programmatic nature. *Music for awhile* exemplifies the
first; *Winter's Song* from the masque of the Four Sea-
sons in the *Fairy Queen*, the second. *Sweeter than
Roses* illustrates his highly individual recitative style.

Source: *Orpheus Britannicus. A Collection of all the
Choicest Songs for One, Two, and Three
Voices compos'd by Mr. Henry Purcell. Together with such Symphonies for Violins or
Flutes, as were by him design'd for any of
them and A Through-Bass to each Song. Figur'd for the Organ, Harpsicord, or Theorbo-
Lute . . . London: Printed by William Pear-
son . . . MDCCXXI. (Third edition.) Book I,
60; II, 26, 126.*

## 47,48 · GABRIEL BATAILLE,

*Eau vive, source d'amour*
and *Qui veut chasser une migraine*

The early development of the solo song took a slightly
different turn in France than in Italy, with the ap-
pearance in the late 16th century of the *airs de cour*,
so called because they were usually performed at one
of the royal or ducal courts of the kingdom. The airs
were composed for solo voice with instrumental accompaniment, usually lute, and were ordinarily of an
amatory nature. The composers showed the same concern as their Italian counterparts in close attention to
the meaning of the words, in florid decoration, and in
somewhat exaggerated emotionalism although this last
somewhat less than the Italians. A less serious but

highly amusing companion piece to the *air de cour*
was the *air à boire*.

Closely associated with the collection and preserva-
tion of these songs was the publisher-composer Gabriel
Bataille (1574–1630); his six anthologies of *airs* were
very popular and several of the volumes were reprinted. In 1617, he was appointed Master of the
Queen's Music and called upon to compose music for
various dramatic representations at court.

The melody of Bataille's setting of some stanzas in
*vers mesurés* attributed to Antoine de Baïf is very
much like that printed by le Père Mersenne in his
chapter on *L'Art de bien chanter* in *Harmonie univer-
selle* (1636) to demonstrate the correct way to sing *vers
mesurés à l'antique*. *Vers mesurés* is the name for an
attempt made by Baïf and others of the *Académie de
poésie et musique* (founded in 1570 by de Baïf and
Jacques Thibaut de Courville) to write lyric verse according to the rules of Latin prosody. This involved
arbitrarily attributing the long and short values to the
French syllables and the corresponding use of notes of
long and short duration in the music, the text determining the form of the music as well as its rhythmic
design. *Eau vive, source d'amour* is one of the few successful attempts to apply this formula. Our transcription is barred to suggest the correct mode of recitation.

*Qui veut chasseur une migraine*, from Batailles'
collection of 1615, is one of the many convivial songs
then popular. They were often sung in parts.

Sources: 47. *III<sup>ème</sup> Livre d'Airs de différents autheurs
mis en tablature de luth par Gabriel Ba-
taille. Paris, P. Ballard, 1611. fol. 65v.*
48. *VI<sup>ème</sup> Livre d'Airs de différents autheurs
mis en tablature de luth par Gabriel
Bataille. Paris, P. Ballard, 1615. fol. 59v.*

## 49 · PIERRE GUÉDRON,

*C'en est fait, je ne verray*

Pierre Guédron (1565–ca. 1621) was a renowned
French singer and composer. In 1590, he was a member of Henri IV's chapel; in 1601 he succeeded Claude
Le Jeune as court composer, and finally, in 1613, he
became *Surintendant de la Musique* under Louis
XIII. He, together with Bataille, Mauduit, Boësset
and others, was responsible for the introduction of
Italian monodic style in French music and also for
many of the ballets so much in favor at the court between 1608–1620. For these he wrote numerous *airs de
cour*, most of which were published in French anthologies with lute accompaniment and in such English
works as Robert Dowland's *A Musicall Banquet*. During his lifetime Guédron enjoyed a very great reputation as a composer; his music shows that he deserved
such esteem. In the matter of recitative and declama-

tory style, Guédron, and after him Lambert, is one of the important precursors of Lully. Guédron's *Déploration* on the death of Henri IV, ded. to the Queen, is in free declamatory style, closely resembling the *recitando* manner employed by the Italian monodists. A *Déploration* may be said to be a vocal counterpart of the instrumental *tombeau*—a kind of musical memorial to a departed person.

*N.B.* M. 6 has only 3 1/2 beats, but m. 10 has 4 1/2 —thus Guédron has equalized the two.

Source: *IV^ème Livre d'Airs de différents autheurs mis en tablature de luth par Gabriel Bataille.* Paris, P. Ballard, 1613.

## 50 · JOACHIM THIBAUT DE COURVILLE,
### *Si je languis d'un martire*

Joachim Thibaut de Courville was one of the founders with Baïf of the *Académie de poésie et de musique* in 1570 (Cf. p. 334). A singer, Courville was a composer as well; however very little of his music is extant. He published no works himself and what does remain is found in collections such as Bataille's anthology from which this piece is taken. It is a true lute song; no polyphonic version exists. The poem, by Philippe Desportes, another member of the Académie, lends itself well to the free declamatory style of Courville's setting, in which the musical rhythm is determined by speech accents rather than harmonic pattern. The written-in graces and ornaments (probably Courville's own) are rarely found and are invaluable for our knowledge of performance practices of the time. In the tablature there is no time signature, nor are there barlines except at the end of sections. In our transcription both time signatures and dotted barlines have been inserted to show more clearly the composer's intentions.

Source: *V^e Livre d'Airs de différents Autheurs mis en tablature de luth par Gabriel Bataille.* Paris, P. Ballard, 1614, (fol. 67v.)

## 51 · SEBASTIEN LE CAMUS,
### *Amour, cruel amour*

Sebastien Le Camus (c. 1610–1677) sang and played the viol in the King's Music of Louis XIV of France. In his official capacity, he was music master to Anne of Austria, to the French Regent (1650) and to Queen Marie Thérèse (1660), so he is referred to as Master of the Queen's Music. Burney writes of him, "Camus is frequently mentioned by French musical writers as one of their best composers of songs of the last century; he was of the King's band and died 1677." (Vol. II, p. 474) The opinion of Le Camus's contemporaries is borne out by the charming rondeau included in this collection.

Source: *Airs à deux et trois parties du feu M. Le Camus, Maistre de la musique de la Reyne.* Paris, Christophe Ballard, 1678.

## 52 · MICHEL LAMBERT,
### *Vous ne sauriez, mes yeux*

Michel Lambert (1610–1696) was lutenist and theorbo player and the most famous singer and singing teacher of the 17th century in France, training many of the best artists for the theatre. He was well liked and an important figure at the court of Louis XIV, occupying the post of *Maître de la musique de chambre du roi.* He collaborated with his son-in-law Lully in the composition and production of several of the famous *ballets de cour.* Lambert was also a prolific composer of songs—he called them *airs*—for several or for single voices, which proved to be immensely popular. They were published in several volumes between 1660 and 1689.

Source: *Les Airs de Monsieur Lambert, maistre de la musique de Chambre du Roy . . .* Paris, 1689.

## 53 · JEAN-BAPTISTE LULLY,
### *Plainte de Vénus par la mort d'Adonis*

The fame of Jean-Baptiste Lully (1632–1687), favorite composer of the Sun King, Louis XIV, rests chiefly upon his dramatic works—ballets, tragedies, comedies —in which he showed himself one of the great masters of his art. His graceful melodic line, his virtuosity at adapting the musical expression exactly to the words, his keen sense of the dramatic, these are some of his merits.

Lully had as collaborators some of the best poets of the time, notably Molière, Benserade, and later, Quinault. With Molière he composed several comedies with incidental music, many ballets with accompanying songs, for some of which he himself wrote the Italian words, as he did also for the ballets in which he collaborated with Benserade and with Quinault. The song here presented, from Benserade's *Ballet de Flore* (1669), amply demonstrates Lully's ability at adapting the musical expression to the literary.

Source: *Ballet royal de Flore,* Coll. Philidor, vol. 16, Bibliothèque du Conservatoire, Paris.

## 54 · MARC-ANTOINE CHARPENTIER,
### *Panis angelicus*

In the early 17th century, King Louis XIV gathered at the French court all the foremost musicians of his realm. The chief of these was Lully, but close behind was Marc-Antoine Charpentier (1636–1704). Charpentier collaborated with Molière by writing music for several of the comédies-ballets, and composed operas in which the Italian influence (he had studied with Carissimi) was clear. He wrote a small treatise on theory; but he is best remembered today for his sacred music, which is considered the most original and striking of the categories of his output. They are mainly extended works—masses, lamentations, motets, sacred histories, canticles and psalms—for voices and instruments, but there are also some of lesser dimensions—hymns, sequences, elevations. The present selection is one of the latter, impressive in its simplicity.

Source: Paris, Bibl. nationale, Oeuvres de M.-A. Charpentier vol. 25, *Meslanges,* no. 10.

### 55 · JEAN-BAPTISTE MOREAU,
*Cantique. Sur les vaines occupations . . .*

Jean-Baptiste Moreau (1656–1733), who began his career in the provinces as a church musician, came to Paris probably some time before 1686. Some time later, by sheer nerve and audacity, he succeeded in getting the Royal Princess to hear him sing one of his own songs. She liked him, and through her he was presented to King Louis XIV and to the formidable Mme. de Maintenon. Moreau wrote some divertissements which were popular, and then established a working relationship with the poet Jean Racine, who was writing two plays to be presented at St. Cyr, the girls' school founded by Mme. de Maintenon. Moreau is considered to be the perfect musical interpreter of Racine's tragedies, but he also wrote other secular and sacred compositions, notable among which are his *Cantiques,* with words by Racine, for the use of the girls of St. Cyr.

Since Lully practically monopolized the opera at that time, Moreau, like others, turned most successfully to other fields—songs, motets, cantiques, divertissements—in which he achieved notable success and popularity. The cantique here presented is the third of a set composed in 1689 for St. Cyr and sung before the King. In it may be observed many of the principles found in Lully's music, especially the correspondence of musical and textual accent and change of meter to fit the declamation of the words more exactly. Although Moreau indicates use of a solo voice and unison chorus, it is possible to sing the entire composition, or any portion thereof, as a solo.

Source: *Cantiques Chantez devant LE ROY, & composez par Monsieur J.-B. Moreau maistre de Musique, & pensionnaire de Sa Majesté. Propres pour les Dames Religieuses, & toutes autres personnes.* Paris, 1695.
*Cantique troisième. Sur les vaines occupations des gens du Siècle. Tiré de divers endroits d'Isaïe & de Jeremie.*

### 56 · SEBASTIEN DE BROSSARD,
Motet: *Qui non diligit Te*

Sébastien de Brossard (1655–1730) was not only a composer, but a bibliophile and lexicographer as well. He gave his collection of books and music to the French nation and it forms the nucleus of the Bibliothèque Nationale's fine music library. He also wrote a *Dictionnaire de musique contenant une explication des terms grecques et latins, italiens et français les plus usités dans la musique* (1703), the first such book to appear in French, indeed one of the first to appear in any language, which had an enormous influence on later works of its kind.

Like another famous musician who lived some fifty years later, J. J. Rousseau, Brossard was an autodidact in music. He was a cleric, connected with the church all his life, and much of his music is sacred, including some very beautiful elevations and motets. However he also composed in quite another vein, his six books of *Airs sérieux et à boire* (1691–1698) containing songs in many moods, some really serious, others jocose. We have chosen as an example of Père Brossard's music one of his solo motets for soprano with basso continuo and two violins.

Source: Uppsala, Universitetsbibliothek. MS Vokal musik i handskrift 5:7.

### 57,58 · CHRISTOPHE BALLARD
and MICHEL PINOLET
DE MONTÉCLAIR,
*Brunetes*

*Brunetes,* simple, unaffected songs, were much in vogue in France at the end of the 17th century and during most of the 18th. Their melodies are graceful and tuneful and their texts usually of a pastoral nature. The term *Brunete* presumably comes from its use in one particular song which enjoyed great popularity in its day. Christophe Ballard published three volumes of *Brunetes, or sentimental little airs with variations and the basso continuo* in 1703, 1704, and 1711. Other books of *Brunetes* were published from time to time by various composers. One of these was Michel Pinolet de Montéclair (1667–1737), who printed *Brunetes anciennes et modernes* about 1716, reworking some of the older songs and adding new variations which could be played on the flute.

We present here Ballard's *Brunete,* as well as Montéclair's version of the same piece. Montéclair has transposed the melody up a fifth; he has also indicated three other transpositions to accomodate high or low voices, thus:

en C.ut          en A.la          en G.sol

Il faut transposer . . . un ton plus bas pour les hauts dessus chantans, & une quarte ou une quinte plus bas pour les bas dessus.

Sources: 57. *Brunetes, ou petits airs tendres avec les doubles et la Basse Continue . . .* (Ballard, Paris, 1703. v. 1, p. 1–6.

   58. *Brunetes anciennes et modernes, I<sup>er</sup> Receuil . . .* Montéclair, Paris, n. d., p. 2–3.

## 59,60 · FRANÇOIS COUPERIN,
*11ème et 12ème Versets du Motet composé de l'ordre du Roy, 1705* and *Doux liens*

François Couperin (1668–1733), called *Couperin le Grand,* was the greatest member of a great musical family. Organist and composer to Louis XIV, *le Roi soleil,* he was associated with such personages as Racine, Corneille, Molière, at the very center of the artistic life of the period. His work reflects the serene dignity and splendor of what has been called the *Grand siècle.* Couperin's most important music is instrumental—the clavecin pieces, *concerts royaux,* organ works—but his religious vocal compositions are also of the highest order. The two Versets from the magnificent motet, using a text from the Psalms, is a fine example of this genre.

His secular vocal compositions must definitely take second place to his instrumental and religious works, nevertheless, his *airs* exemplify the sophisticated simplicity and gentle grace that characterize the 17th-century *air de cour* and the semi-popular *brunetes.* One should not be deceived by the simple, almost naive quality of these little pieces; in Couperin's time, the singer was expected to add subtly stylized ornamentation beyond that indicated, thus imparting an expressiveness and emotionalism that is not apparent in the formal framework. Couperin wrote only three *airs sérieux; Doux liens* is the second of these, published in 1701. The text is a translation of an Italian poem which had been previously set by A. Scarlatti.

Sources: 59. *Sept Versets du Motet composé de l'ordre du Roy Par Monsieur Couperin,* Organiste de la Chapelle de Sa Majesté . . . Et chanté à Versilles le—Mars, 1705. A Paris. Chez Christophe Ballard, 1705.

   60. R. Ballard, *Airs sérieux et à boire.* Paris, 1701.

## 61 · LOUIS-NICHOLAS CLÉRAMBAULT,
*Monarque redouté* from *Orphée*

Closely associated with the French court was Louis-Nicholas Clérambault (1676–1749), *surintendant de la musique* in the service of the king's formidable mistress Mme. de Maintenon, who founded the famous girls' school at St. Cyr. Clérambault wrote for this institution and was also organist successively at the churches of St. Louis, St. Cyr and at Saint-Sulpice. He wrote much music in this capacity and has been compared with Couperin Le Grand as composer for organ and dubbed the last really significant composer in the great classical tradition. Several pieces for the stage, which cannot correctly be called operas, are preserved. But Clérambault's most important and significant works are his cantatas, for which he displayed a very special talent. Between 1710 and 1726 he wrote five books of cantatas, both sacred and secular, and often to texts dealing with the characters of classical mythology. Such was his *Orphée,* for solo voice, considered by many to be his masterpiece. Our selection from this work is its high point, Orpheus's plea to Pluto. In its lyric eloquence it brings to mind Gluck's music composed for the same story some fifty years later.

Source: *Cantates françoises à I, et II. voix, Avec Simphonie, et sans Simphonie, composées par M<sup>r</sup> Clérambault . . . Livre Premier. . . .* Paris, 1710. (Cantate troisième, *Orphée.*)

## 62 · ANDRÉ CAMPRA,
Two airs from *L'Europe Galant*

In spite of his Italian name, André Campra (1660–1744) was completely French. Born at Aix-en-Provence, he showed a genius for music early and occupied posts in various provincial towns before he came to Paris in 1694. Here, he fell in love with the theatre and found that he had a very special talent for writing for it. After the success of his two "opéra ballets" *L'Europe galante* (1697) and *Le Carnaval de Venise* (1699), he resigned from the church to devote himself exclusively to the threatre, producing some forty-three works, including several tragedies. Of interest are his *spectacles coupés,* entertainments made up of scenes taken from several operas, presented as one performance; also his *pasticcios* of music by other composers, using airs and scenes from their works. His *Fragments de Lully* was especially appreciated.

Campra, in addition to his theatrical works, wrote three books of *Cantates françaises,* a number of motets, a Mass and two books of Psalms. He has been rated as the most remarkable French dramatic composer between Lully and Rameau. His works were popular for many years.

We present here two little Airs from the *2ème Entrée* of his greatest success, *L'Europe galante.* They distantly recall the earlier *air de cour* and show, once again, how strong in French musical tradition is the deceptively simple, elegant air for solo voice.

Source: *L'Europe Galante, Ballet, représenté en l'an 1697. par l'académie royale de musique; De la Composition de Monsieur Campra, Maitre de Musique de la Chapelle du Roy . . .* Paris,

J.-B.-C. Ballard, 1724. (From Deuxième Entrée, sc. iii. mm. 125–157.)

## 63 · THOMAS SELLE,
*Amarilli, du schönstes Bild*

Thomas Selle (1599–1663) was German-born and German-trained at Leipzig's Thomasschule and at the University. After holding various ecclesiastical positions in north Germany, he finally came to Hamburg in 1637. In 1641 he became town Cantor and head of the music at the Hamburg Cathedral. His close association with the poet Johann Rist resulted in a long-continued collaboration. Selle was a prolific composer of sacred music and of secular songs. The present selection is from *Monophonetica*, a volume of gay and lively lieder for solo voice in the style of French and Italian chansons.

Source: *Monophonetica, h. e. Allerhand lustige und anmutige Frewden-Liedlein mit nur einen Vocal Stimme zum Basso Continuum in eine Theorb; Laute; Clavicymbel; Regal: &c lieblich zu singen gesetzt . . . Hamburg, 1636.*

## 64 · HEINRICH ALBERT,
*Mein liebstes Seelchen*

Heinrich Albert (1604–1651) was a poet as well as musician. Although he received his early musical training from his cousin, Heinrich Schütz in Dresden, he was not originally directed toward the art of music and was sent to the university to study Law. He abandoned this study and became organist at the Königsberg Cathedral, where he and his music were much admired. He was a member of the Königsberg poets' circle, both writing verses himself and setting them and poems by others of the group to music. Two of the best poets of the circle, Simon Dach and Robert Roberthin, furnished him with many texts. This group met regularly for social activities in which music and poetry played a large part. Albert wrote hymns, motets, even an opera, but his fame rests on his continuo songs, the *Arien*, which he brought out in eight parts between 1638 and 1650. These unpretentious works were so popular that they appeared in many pirated and illicit editions. Most of his songs are very simple, strophic pieces, often with instrumental ritornellos, most likely intended for evenings of informal entertainment.

Source: *Erster Teil der Arien oder Melodeien etlicher teils geistlicher, teils weltlicher, zu guten Sitten und Lust dienender Lieder. In ein Positiv, Klavizimbel, Theorbe oder anders vollstimmig Instrument zu singen gesetzt,* Königsberg, 1638. No. 13.

## 65 · HEINRICH SCHÜTZ,
*Ich liege und schlafe* [SWV 310]

Heinrich Schütz (1585–1672), one of the greatest of German composers, spent most of his long career at the court of Saxony. A young aristocrat of broad culture, he decided to devote himself to music and at the age of twenty-four, with the help of the Elector of Saxony, went to Venice where he studied under the famous master Giovanni Gabrieli. Schütz was profoundly influenced by Gabrieli and perhaps also by Monteverdi. From them, he adopted the new Italian style of highly expressive music, merging this style with his deep German culture and his earnest German religious faith.

Among the items in his musical production of particular interest to us are his *Kleine geistliche Koncerten,* simple compositions for one or more solo voices with continuo, perhaps written for domestic use. They often contain directions for the artists, a rarity at this time. The songs in the *Koncerten* show Schütz's mastery of melody, his subtle phrasing to bring out the full meaning of the text, and his economy of musical means to get a maximum effect. They are all composed upon texts from the German Bible.

Source: *Kleine Geistlichen Concerten. Mit 1.2.3.4 und 5 Stimmen sampt bey gefügten Basso Continuo vor die Orgell. In die Musik übersetzt durch Henricum Sagittarien. . . . 1639*

## 66 · ANDREAS HAMMERSCHMIDT,
*Sarabande. Glückselig Rosilis*

The renowned organist and composer Andreas Hammerschmidt (1612–1675) was Bohemian by birth but spent most of his life in Germany, serving as organist in Freiburg in Saxony from 1635 until 1639, and in Zittau from 1639 until his death. A prolific composer, he wrote in most of the forms then current. His most important works are those for voices and instruments in the concerted Italian style similar to, and perhaps modelled on, the compositions of Heinrich Schütz. He is important in connection with the development of Lutheran church music before Bach and many of his chorale melodies are still in use today. While most of his works were intended for church use, he wrote also in secular style, including two sets of dance pieces among his early compositions. We also find dance forms used often in his vocal works, as may be seen in this song in form of a sarabande.

Source: *Dritter Theil Geist-und Weltliche Oden und Madrigalien Mit 1.2.3.4. und 5. Stimmen nebenst dem Basso Continuo in die Music versetzt.* Leipzig, In Verlegung Heinrich Nerliche. 1649. No. 13.

## 67 · ADAM KRIEGER,
### *Fleug, Psyche, fleug*

Adam Krieger (1634–1666) spent all his life and career 'in northern Germany, chiefly at the court of Saxony, where he held the post of organist to the Elector. A pupil of Heinrich Schütz, he was in the main stream of German music during the first half of the 17th century. He is remembered nowadays almost exclusively for his *Arien*, songs for one or more voices with continuo accompaniment. They are characterized by a certain folk quality and an elegance of phrasing which is partly due to the fact that Krieger was a poet as well as a composer. Very often he added an instrumental ritornello at the end of each strophe.

*Fleug, Psyche, fleug*, an epithalamium, is of large dimensions, in reality a little cantata in the then new Italian style.

Source: *Neue Arien in 6. Zehen eingetheilet von Einer, Zwo, Drey und Fünf-Vocal-Stimmen benebenst ihren Ritornellen, auf Zwey Violinen, Zwey Violen, und einem Violon, sammt dem Basso continuo, zu Singen und zu Spielen. So nach seinem Seel. Tode erst zusammen gebracht und zum andern mahl zum Druck befördert werden.* Dresden, Hübner, 1676. Aria 8: Das vierte Zehn.

## 68 · PHILIPP HEINRICH ERLEBACH,
### *Kommt, ihr Stunden*

Philipp Heinrich Erlebach (1657–1714) was best known to his contemporaries as an instrumental composer and has a definite place in the history of the sonata. However, he was also a prolific writer of vocal music, mainly of a religious nature. He was born at Esens in Friedland and spent most of his long career at that city and at the court of Rudolstadt, where he occupied the post of *Hofkapellmeister*.

He stated that he never went to France, but there is clear evidence of French influence, especially of Lully, in his vocal works. Only a small portion of his large production has been published, and much of it is lost. His most renowned published vocal work was *Harmonische Freude Musicalischer Freunde*, a collection of "moral and political arias" which appeared in 1697, a second set following in 1710.

Source: *Harmonische Freude Musicalische Freunde Erster Theil—Fünfzig Moralisch-und Politischen Arien, nebst zugehörigen Ritornellen à II Violini & Basso-Continuo.* Nürnberg, gedruckt bey Christian Sigmund Froberg, 1697. (No. 49).

## 69 · FRIEDRICH WILHELM ZACHOW,
### *Ruhe, Friede, Freud' und Wonne*

Friedrich Wilhelm Zachow (or Zachau) (1663–1712), was organist of the church of Our Lady in Halle from 1684 until his death. Although he is remembered for having been the young Handel's first teacher, his works have almost been forgotten and neglected. He was in fact a thoroughly competent musician whose compositions are written with taste and style and a certain serious grace. A large collection of his compositions exists in manuscript: works for organ, church cantatas and other items for church service. The aria printed here is taken from the cantata *Ruhe, Friede, Freud' und Wonne* for Pentecost.

Source: Berlin, Staatsbibliothek MS fol. 23,445, no. 4.
Pr. *Denkmäler der deutscher Tonkunst* XXI–XXII, p. 55.

## 70 · JOHANN THEIL(E),
### *Jesu, mein Herr und Gott*

Johann Theil(e) (1646–1724) spent his entire life in north Germany. He was known during his career as a theorist—his contemporaries called him "the father of counterpoint"—but he was also a singer and a virtuoso on the viola da gamba. He studied briefly with Heinrich Schütz. Theile settled for a period in Hamburg, and wrote the first opera performed in the new opera house, a *Singspiel* on a biblical subject entitled *Adam und Eva, oder der erschaffene, gefallene und wieder aufgerichtete Mensch* (Adam and Eve, or Man, created, fallen, and redeemed.) The text is still extant but the music has disappeared.

Theile wrote mainly church music: several masses, a St. Matthew Passion, sacred cantatas and motets for solo voice. The present selection is one of the latter. Only two books of Theile's music were printed during his lifetime, and most of his work remains in manuscript.

Source: Uppsala Universitets bibliotek, Vok. mus. i hdskr. 35:18.

## 71 · REINHARD KEISER,
### *Per compiacerti, o cara*
### from *L'inganno fedele*

Reinhard Keiser (1674–1739), noted bon-vivant, talented impresario, excellent performer on the organ, was at the same time a composer of genius. All of his career was spent in north Germany. He settled first in Brunswick, where his first operas were produced, and in 1697 moved to Hamburg to become director and chief composer of the Opera in 1703. He wrote opera after opera, sometimes as many as four a year. The number of his dramatic works is not quite certain, but one hundred is a conservative estimate. The texts were in German or Italian, and with his smooth and graceful melodies Keiser helped to introduce the Italian style into Germany. He is said to have originated the famous "winter concerts" at which the best and most attractive performers played and sang fine music, the soirée being concluded by a magnificent banquet, all for the price of one ticket.

Very little of his music has been published in modern editions, despite the fact that the scores for at least thirty-three of his operas exist as well as a number of vocal collections and sacred works. *Per compiacerti,* a *Siciliana,* is from *L'inganno fedele,* originally an opera but later published as a *pastorale,* in which shortened form it exists today.

Source: *Erlesene Sätze aus der Opera L'Inganno Fedele Bestehend in Sing-Sachen für verschiedene Stimmen . . . Hamburg, 1714.*

## 72 · GEORGE FRIDERIC HANDEL, *Il gelsomino* [Cantata No. 63]

George Frideric Handel (1685–1759), although German by birth, resided in England from 1711 until his death. He wrote mainly in the Italian style, but with his own personal touch. His vast production includes serenatas, cantatas, choral works, organ and harpsichord pieces, instrumental suites, in addition to operas and oratorios. He, like Bach, was a giant and needs no introduction.

Handel's cantatas, most of them composed early in his career, number exactly one hundred (seventy-two for solo voice with basso continuo and twenty-eight with orchestral accompaniment). The Italian cantatas, like those of Bach, are not well-known and merit greater familiarity. They are very important in the formation of his style, having been written about 1708 or 1709 and modelled on those of the Italians, including A. Scarlatti, G. A. Perti, Giovanni Bononcini and others.

*Il gelsomino,* for soprano, consists of two arias linked by a recitative and shows clearly Handel's adoption of Italian style, especially in the lilting Siciliana rhythm of the second aria.

Source: *The Works of George Frideric Handel,* edited by Friedrich Chrysander. Printed for the German Handel Society. Leipzig, 1887? Vol. 51, no. 63.

## 73 · JOHANN SEBASTIAN BACH, Recitative: *Wir beten zu dem Tempel an* and Aria: *Höchster, mache deine Güte* [BWV 51]

J. S. Bach (1685–1750), the great German master, needs little introduction today. His great orchestral suites, the *Well-Tempered Clavier,* the mighty organ works, the St. Matthew Passion are known to all. Of his nearly two hundred sacred cantatas, few are familiar today, yet that form was one in which he was most prolific. Bach's cantatas were an outgrowth of the Italian cantata, but in his hands they acquired a form peculiar to the needs of the Lutheran liturgy. His secular cantatas do not differ in construction from the sacred ones, except for the absence of chorales.

The cantata from which this recitative and aria are taken is BWV No. 51, *Jauchzet Gott in alle Landen,* written for the 15th Sunday after Trinity "et in ogni tempo." The author of the text is not known and the date of composition is uncertain, although some authorities give 1730. The soprano part exists in Bach's own autograph.

This recitative, which breaks into an *arioso,* and its companion aria form the second and third sections of the cantata. They are superb examples of late Baroque ornamented style.

Source: Bach Gesellschaft Ausgabe, XII: ii, p. 3 ff.

## 74 · JOHANN ADOLPHE HASSE, *Orgoglioso fiumicello* from the cantata *L'inciampo*

Probably no composer has ever been more successful or more idolized during his lifetime than Johann Adolphe Hasse (1699–1783), not only in his native Germany, in England and in Austria, but in his adopted country Italy, where he was known affectionately as "il caro Sassone." He had a fine tenor voice, was a virtuoso on the harpsichord, and had the good fortune to be married to one of the greatest *prime donne* of the century, Faustina Bordoni. A pupil of Porpora and Alessandro Scarlatti at Naples, he immediately adopted the Italian style for his operas, of which he wrote fifty-six during his lifetime. By a great stroke of fortune, he early came into contact with the greatest operatic librettist of all time, Pietro Metastasio, and the two collaborated in many popular works. Hasse also wrote a great deal of church music, oratorios, intermezzi, serenatas, and about twenty cantatas, some with full orchestral accompaniment. His cantata *L'inciampo* is for solo soprano with basso continuo and is written to a text by Metastasio.

Source: British Museum, Add MSS 31604, 14213, and 14229.
  (According to MS 14229, the date of the work is 1732).

## 75 · JOHANNES SIGISMUND SCHOLZ (Sperontes), *Ich bin nun wie ich bin*

One of the most widely circulated and famous song collections of the 18th century was *Die Singende Muse an der Pleisse,* published in 1736 by Sperontes, pseudonym of the poet Johannes Sigismund Scholz (1705–1750). This work consisted of one hundred odes, poetic texts set to pre-existing music—dances, clavier pieces, airs of all kinds. The collection was so popular that supplements were brought out in 1742, 1743, and 1745, and all the fascicles were reprinted frequently. The contents reflect accurately the taste of the time and preserve a repertory that has long since disappeared. One of the composition types included in it was the *Murky,* which enjoyed considerable vogue up through Beethoven's time. This form is characterized by broken octaves in the bass and a lively rhythm. One of the eleven Murkys in *Die Singende Muse* is given here.

Source: *Sperontes, Singende Muse an der Pleisse in 2. mahl 50 Oden, der neuesten und besten musicalischen Stücke mit den darzu gehörigen Melodien zu beliebter Clavier-Übung und Gemüths–Ergötzung . . . Leipzig, 1736. (No. 33).*

# *Index*

First lines of songs are in italics.
Boldface page references indicate historical material.
Names of composers included in this anthology are in caps
     and small caps.
Song titles are in quotes.